Book Title: Computer Security Division 2011 Annual Report

Book Author: Patrick D. O'Reilly;

Book Abstract: Title III of the E-Government Act of 2002, entitled the Federal Information Security Management Act (FISMA) of 2002, requires NIST to prepare an annual public report on activities undertaken in the previous year, and planned for the coming year, to carry out responsibilities under this law. The primary goal of the Computer Security Division (CSD), a component of NIST s Information Technology Laboratory (ITL), is to provide standards and technology that protects information systems against threats to the confidentiality, integrity, and availability of information and services. During Fiscal Year 2011 (FY 2011), CSD successfully responded to numerous challenges and opportunities in fulfilling that mission. Through CSD's diverse research agenda and engagement in many national priority initiatives, high-quality, cost-effective security and privacy mechanisms were developed and applied that improved information security across the federal government and the greater information security community. This annual report highlights the research agenda and activities in which CSD was engaged during FY 2011.

Citation: NIST Interagency/Internal Report (NISTIR) - 7816

Keywords: Federal Information Security Management Act; FISMA, Computer Security Division; CSD; Information Security

NIST
National Institute of
Standards and Technology
U.S. Department of Commerce

Table of Contents

The United States (U.S.) economy and U.S. citizens are reliant on information technology (IT). Federal agencies and the private sector cannot function without IT. Protecting IT, including its information and the information infrastructure, is critical for the Nation. The Computer Security Division (CSD), a component of the Information Technology Laboratory at the National Institute of Standards and Technology (NIST) is responsible for developing standards, guidelines, tests and metrics for the protection of non-national security federal information and information systems. The CSD standards, guidelines, tests and metrics have also become leading resources for information security in the private sector.

During fiscal year 2011 (FY2011), CSD extended its research and development agenda for high-quality, cost-effective security and privacy mechanisms to foster improved information security across the federal government and the greater information security community. This included addressing challenges for the protection of information and information systems for enterprise environments as well as in cloud computing and mobile infrastructures. In addition, we explored processes and mechanisms to protect personally identifiable information through the application of privacy controls and privacy-enhancing technologies. Our research also extended to non-traditional forms of IT including cyber-physical systems and security for sensor devices.

Our ability to interact with the broad federal community continues to be critical to our success. This interaction helps to ensure that our research is consistent with national objectives related to or impacted by information security. This interaction is most prominent in our strengthened collaborations with the Department of Defense, the Intelligence Community, and the Committee on National Security Systems to establish a common foundation for information security across the federal government. The FY2011 release of Special Publication 800-39, *Managing Information Security Risk: Organization, Mission, and Information System View*, developed by the Joint Task Force Transformation Initiative Interagency Working Group, is not only leading to more uniform and consistent ways to manage risks, but it is also providing a strong basis for greater information sharing among stakeholders.

The success of many of our technical programs is dependent on our partnership with industry. In FY2011, we continued to drive greater adoption of security automation protocols by major information technology manufacturers, as well as new and innovative applications of security automation to more diverse use cases including continuous monitoring and health information technology. Lower in the stack, CSD worked with the computer hardware industry on mechanisms to improve security at the hardware layer. Recently issued guidelines on protecting the BIOS in laptop and desktop computers have already had a major impact with several hardware vendors offering products intended to meet the guidelines, laying the foundation for more secure systems.

Other significant highlights of our work in FY2011 include NIST's leadership role in supporting the establishment of the Federal Risk and Authorization Management Program (FedRAMP), which facilitates a standard approach for provisional security automation of cloud computing products and services; and in hosting the third round of the SHA-3 competition to determine a successor to the current government-approved cryptographic hash algorithm.

For many years, the Computer Security Division (CSD) has made great contributions to help secure the nation's sensitive information and information systems. Looking forward to FY2012, CSD will continue to lead in areas as diverse as risk management and continuous monitoring, awareness and outreach, privacy-enhancing cryptography, security for virtual environments, and mobile computing technology security. CSD will also focus on aligning our resources to not only develop and apply innovative security technologies, but also to enhance our ability to address current and future computer and information security challenges faced by critical national and international priorities.

Donna Dodson
Chief, Computer Security Division
& Deputy Chief Cybersecurity Advisor

Division Organization

Donna Dodson
Chief, Computer Security Division and
Deputy Chief Cybersecurity Advisor

Matthew Scholl
Deputy Division Chief

GROUP MANAGERS

David Ferraiolo
Systems and Emerging Technologies
Security Research Group

Matthew Scholl
Security Management and
Assurance Group

Tim Polk
Cryptographic Technology
Group

The E-Government Act, Public Law 107-347, passed by the 107th Congress and signed into law by the President in December 2002, recognized the importance of information security to the economic and national security interests of the United States. Title III of the E-Government Act, entitled the Federal Information Security Management Act (FISMA) of 2002, included duties and responsibilities for the National Institute of Standards and Technology, Information Technology Laboratory (ITL), Computer Security Division (CSD). In 2011, CSD addressed its assignments through the following projects and activities:

- Issued 17 final NIST Special Publications (SPs) that provided management, operational, and technical security guidance in areas such as: Basic Input/Output System (BIOS) protection, cloud computing, configuration management, cryptography, industrial control system security, information security continuous monitoring, key management, security automation, and virtualization. In addition, 19 draft SPs on a variety of topics, including: cloud computing, cryptographic key management, electronic authentication, personal identity verification, and risk assessments, were issued for public comment;

- Continued the successful collaboration with the Office of the Director of National Intelligence, Committee on National Security Systems, and the Department of Defense to establish a common foundation for information security across the federal government, including a consistent process for selecting and specifying safeguards and countermeasures (i.e., security controls) for federal information systems;

- Provided assistance to agencies and the private sector: conducted ongoing, substantial reimbursable and non-reimbursable assistance support, including many outreach efforts such as the Federal Information Systems Security Educators' Association (FISSEA), the Federal Computer Security Program Managers' Forum (FCSM Forum), and the Small Business Corner;

- Reviewed security policies and technologies from the private sector and national security systems for potential federal agency use: hosted a growing repository of federal agency security practices, public/private security practices, and security configuration checklists for Information Technology (IT) products. Continued to lead, in conjunction with the Government of Canada's Communications Security Establishment, the Cryptographic Module Validation Program (CMVP). The Common Criteria Evaluation and Validation Scheme (CCEVS) and CMVP facilitate security testing of IT products usable by the federal government;

- Solicited recommendations of the Information Security and Privacy Advisory Board on draft standards and guidelines and on information security and privacy issues regularly at quarterly meetings;

- Provided outreach, workshops, and briefings: conducted ongoing awareness briefings and outreach to CSD's customer community and beyond to ensure comprehension of guidance and awareness of planned and future activities. CSD also held workshops to identify areas that the customer community wishes to be addressed, and to scope guidelines in a collaborative and open format; and

- Produced an annual report as a NIST Interagency Report (NISTIR). The 2003-2010 Annual Reports are available via our Computer Security Resource Center (CSRC) website.

Security Management and Assurance Group

Strategic Goal

The Security Management and Assurance (SMA) Group provides leadership, expertise, outreach, validation, standards, and guidelines to assist the federal IT community in protecting information and information systems, and in using these critical assets to accomplish federal agency missions.

Overview

Information security is an integral element of good management. Information and information systems are critical assets that support the mission of an organization. Protecting these information assets can be as important as protecting other organizational resources, such as intellectual property, physical assets, or employees. Organizations need to have assurance that the security practices and technologies that they implement provide adequate security necessary to protect their mission, systems, and information.

Ultimate responsibility for the success of an organization lies with its senior management. These officials establish the organization's information security program and its overall program goals, objectives, and priorities in order to support the mission of the organization. They are also responsible for ensuring that required resources are applied to the program.

Collaboration with other organizations is critical for success. Within the federal government, NIST collaborates with the Office of Management and Budget (OMB), the Government Accountability Office (GAO), and all Executive Branch agencies. We also work closely with a number of information technology organizations and standards bodies, as well as with public and private organizations. Internationally we work jointly with the governments of our allies, including Canada, Japan, Australia, and several European and Asian countries, to standardize and validate the correct implementation of cryptography.

Major initiatives in this area include:

- The Federal Information Security Management Act (FISMA) implementation project;
- The Cryptographic Module Validation Program (CMVP);
- The Cryptographic Algorithm Validation Program (CAVP);
- Security for Health Information Technology;
- Security standards and conformance for the nation's Smart Grid;
- The National Initiative for Cybersecurity Education (NICE);
- Extended outreach initiatives to federal and nonfederal agencies, state and local governments, international organizations, and small businesses;
- Standards development; and
- Producing and updating NIST Special Publications (SPs) on security management topics.

Key to the success in this area is our ability to interact with a broad constituency – federal and nonfederal – in order to ensure that our program is consistent with national objectives related to or impacted by information security.

Federal Information Security Management Act

FISMA Implementation Project – Phase I

Phase I of the FISMA Implementation Project focuses on developing a comprehensive series of standards and guidelines to help federal agencies build strong cybersecurity programs, defend against increasingly sophisticated cyber attacks, and demonstrate compliance to security requirements set forth in legislation, Executive Orders, Homeland Security Directives, and OMB polices. During 2010-2011, CSD strengthened its collaboration with the Department of Defense, the Intelligence Community, and the Committee on National Security Systems, in partnership with the Joint Task Force Transformation Initiative, which continues to develop key cybersecurity guidelines for protecting federal information and information systems for the Unified Information Security Framework. Previously, the Joint Task Force developed common security guidance in the critical areas of security controls for information systems and organizations, security assessment procedures to demonstrate security control effectiveness, security authorizations for risk acceptance decisions, and continuous monitoring activities to ensure that decision makers receive the most up-to-date information on the security state of their information systems.

In FY2011, CSD worked on the following initiatives:

(i) *Risk Management and Risk Assessment Guidance:* Developed a three-tiered risk management approach for enterprise-wide use focusing on an *organization* level, *mission/business process* level, and *information system* level. Developed a four-step risk management process that is applied across all three risk management tiers and that includes risk framing, risk assessment, risk response, and risk monitoring. Provided comprehensive risk assessment guidance examining the relationships among key risk factors including threats, vulnerabilities, impact, and likelihood.

(ii) *Continuous Monitoring and Configuration Management Guidelines:* Developed information security continuous monitoring guidelines to help organizations determine the effectiveness of deployed security controls, changes to organizational information systems and environments of operation, and compliance with federal legislation, policies, directives, standards, and guidance. Developed security configuration management guidelines to ensure that organizations employ effective techniques to manage information technology components and implement required configuration settings within information technology products, thereby reducing or eliminating classes of threats to organizational information systems and organizations.

(iii) *FISMA Outreach Activity to Public and Private Sector Organizations:* Conducted cybersecurity outreach briefings and provided support to state and local governments as well as private sector organizations. Briefings included key cybersecurity topics of interest, such as effective implementation of the NIST Risk Management Framework. In addition, conducted outreach activities with academic institutions, providing information on NIST's security standards and guidelines and exploring new areas of cybersecurity research and development.

In FY2011, CSD completed the following activities in cooperation and collaboration with its Joint Task Force partners:

- Developed NIST Special Publication (SP) 800-39, *Managing Information Security Risk: Organization, Mission, and Information System View*; and

- Developed an initial public draft of SP 800-30, Revision 1, *Guide for Conducting Risk Assessments*.

In FY2012, CSD intends to:

- Update SP 800-53, Revision 3, *Recommended Security Controls for Federal Information Systems and Organizations*, to Revision 4;

- Finalize SP 800-30, Revision 1, *Guide for Conducting Risk Assessments;*

- Develop an information system security and engineering guideline; and

- Expand cybersecurity outreach program to include additional state, local, and tribal governments as well as private sector organizations and academic institutions.

---

http://csrc.nist.gov/sec-cert
Contact:
Dr. Ron Ross
(301) 975-5390
ron.ross@nist.gov

FISMA Implementation Project – Phase II

Phase II of the FISMA Implementation Project focuses on building common understanding and reference guides for organizations applying the NIST suite of publications that support the Risk Management Framework (RMF), and for public and private sector organizations that provide security assessments of information systems for federal agencies. Security assessments determine the extent to which the security controls are implemented correctly, operating as intended, and producing the desired outcome with respect to meeting the security requirements for the system. Management, operational, and technical security controls, as well as information technology products and services used in security control implementation, are included in security assessments.

In FY2011, CSD worked on the following initiatives:

(i) *Training:* Developed classroom-based and web-based training courses, published Quick Start Guides (QSGs), and developed Frequently Asked Questions (FAQs) for establishing common understanding of the NIST standards and guidelines supporting the RMF.

(ii) *Organizational Security Assessment Capability:* Defined minimum capability and proficiency criteria for public and private sector organizations providing security assessment services for federal agencies.

In FY2011, CSD completed the following activities:

- Developed final drafts of web-based and classroom-based training courses on the RMF, *Applying the RMF to Federal Information Systems*;

- Developed draft of web-based training course for the Monitor step of the six-step RMF;

- Completed second draft QSGs and FAQs supporting the Select step of the six-step RMF (adding to the currently available QSGs and FAQs for the Categorize and Monitor steps); and

- Developed technical capability requirements and proficiency test scenarios for organizations to demonstrate their capability in providing security assessments of cloud-based information systems consistent with FISMA and NIST standards and guidelines. The technical capability requirements were derived from Draft NIST Interagency Report (NISTIR) 7328, *Assessment Provider Requirements and Customer Responsibilities: Building a Security Assessment Credentialing Program for Federal Information Systems*, and the core set of NIST standards and guidelines from Phase I of the FISMA Implementation Project that support the RMF. CSD is collaborating with the ITL Systems and Software Division (SSD) and the NIST Standards Coordination Office using the International Standard ISO/IEC 17020:2008 *General criteria for the operation of various types of bodies performing inspections*, in supporting the General Services Administration (GSA) for qualifying security assessment organizations (SAOs) to conduct security assessments of Cloud Service Providers (CSPs) cloud-based information systems.

In FY2012, CSD intends to:

- Develop final draft QSGs and FAQs for the Implement, Assess, and Authorize steps of the six-step RMF; and

- Prototype the proficiency test capability demonstration in supporting GSA for qualifying SAOs to conduct security assessments of cloud-based information systems.

http://csrc.nist.gov/sec-cert
Contacts:

Mr. Arnold Johnson
(301) 975-3247
arnold.johnson@nist.gov

Ms. Pat Toth
(301) 975-5140
patricia.toth@nist.gov

Computer Security Resource Center (CSRC)

The Computer Security Resource Center (CSRC) is CSD's website and is one of the most visited websites at NIST. CSRC encourages broad sharing of information security tools and practices, provides a resource for information security standards and guidelines, and identifies and links key security web resources to support industry and government users. CSRC is an integral component of all of the work that we conduct and produce. It is our repository for anyone, public or private sector, wanting to access our documents and other valuable information security-related information. During FY2011, our division's two websites, CSRC and the National Vulnerability Database (NVD), had more than 102.6 million requests combined[1]. CSRC received a little over 54.0 million total requests. The NVD website within CSRC received over 48.6 million total requests.

TOTAL NUMBER OF WEBSITE REQUESTS: CSRC & NVD

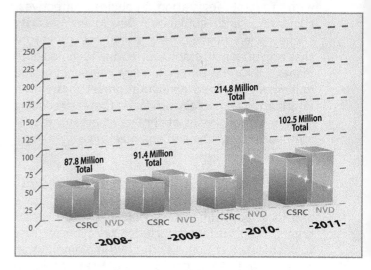

CSRC is the primary gateway for gaining access to NIST computer security publications, standards, and guidelines, and serves as a vital link to our internal and external customers. The following documents can be found on CSRC: Drafts for public comment, Federal Information Processing Standards (FIPS), Special Publications (SPs), NIST Interagency Reports (NISTIRs), and ITL Security Bulletins.

The URL for the Publications homepage is: http://csrc.nist.gov/publications. Publications are organized by Topic, Family categories, and Legal Requirements to help users locate relevant information quickly.

---

[1] These statistics are based from October 1, 2010 to September 30, 2011 time frame. The total requests consist of web pages and file downloads.

During FY2011, the top ten downloaded publications were:

1. SP 800-53 Revision 3, *Recommended Security Controls for Federal Information Systems and Organizations*;

2. SP 800-30, *Risk Management Guide for Information Technology Systems*;

3. SP 800-77, *Guide to IPsec VPNs*;

4. SP 800-100, *Information Security Handbook: A Guide for Managers*;

5. SP 800-94, *Guide to Intrusion Detection and Prevention Systems (IDPS)*;

6. SP 800-61 Revision 1, Computer *Security Incident Handling Guide*;

7. FIPS 140-2, *Security Requirements for Cryptographic Modules*;

8. SP 800-53A, *Guide for Assessing the Security Controls in Federal Information Systems*;

9. SP 800-12, *An Introduction to Computer Security: The NIST Handbook*;

10. SP 800-92, *Guide to Computer Security Log Management*.

The CSRC is continuously updated with new information on various project pages. Some of the major highlights of CSRC during FY2011 were:

- Continuous updates to the National Initiative for Cybersecurity Education (NICE) website, which includes: 2011 NICE Workshop, the NICE Strategic Plan (Draft), and the NICE Framework. URL: http://www.nist.gov/nice;

- Creation and updates of new validated products and certificate web pages for the Cryptographic Module Validation Program (CMVP) and Cryptographic Algorithm Validation Program (CAVP);

- Webcasts provided for the ISPAB quarterly meetings; and

- Updates made for the Access Control Policy Tool (ACPT) web pages, to name a few of the CSRC updates performed during FY2011.

In addition to CSRC, CSD maintains a publication announcement mailing list. This is a free email list that notifies subscribers about publications that have been posted to the CSRC website. This email list is a valuable tool for more than 12,000 subscribers including federal government employees, the private sector, educational institutions, and individuals with a personal interest in information technology (IT) security. Subscribers are notified when CSD releases a publication, posts an announcement on CSRC, or when the CSD is hosting a security event. Individuals who are interested in learning more about this list or subscribing to it should visit this web page on CSRC for more information: http://csrc.nist.gov/publications/subscribe.html.

Questions on the website should be sent to the CSRC Webmaster at: webmaster-csrc@nist.gov.

Contact:
Mr. Patrick O'Reilly
(301) 975-4751
patrick.oreilly@nist.gov

Federal Computer Security Program Managers' Forum

The Federal Computer Security Program Managers' Forum is a group that is sponsored by NIST to promote the sharing of security-related information among federal agencies. The Forum, which serves more than 1,042 members, strives to provide an ongoing opportunity for managers of federal information security programs to exchange information security materials in a timely manner, build upon the experiences of other programs, and reduce possible duplication of effort. It provides a mechanism for NIST to share information directly with federal agency information security program managers in fulfillment of NIST's leadership mandate under FISMA. It also assists NIST in establishing and maintaining relationships with other individuals or organizations that are actively addressing information security issues within the federal government. NIST serves as the Secretariat of the Forum, providing necessary administrative and logistical support. Kevin Stine serves as the Chairperson for the Forum. Participation in Forum meetings is open to federal government employees who participate in the management of their organization's information security program. There are no membership dues.

The Forum hosts the Federal Agency Security Practices (FASP) website, maintains an extensive email list, and holds bimonthly meetings and an annual two-day conference to discuss current issues and developments of interest to those responsible for protecting sensitive (unclassified) federal systems. The Forum plays a valuable role in helping NIST and other federal agencies develop and maintain a strong, proactive stance in the identification and resolution of new strategic and tactical IT security issues as they emerge.

Topics of discussion at Forum meetings in FY2011 included briefings from various federal agencies on: Federal Virtual

Training Environment (FedVTE) and Federal Cybersecurity Training Exercise (FedCTE), and Supply Chain Risk Management; FISMA Annual Reporting Process Report and Continuous Monitoring; Security Automation Roadmap and Managed Trusted Internet Protocol Service (MTIPS) Experience and Lessons Learned; and the NIST Mobile Application Security and Department of Justice (DOJ) Mobility Program. The April meeting, held at the National Oceanic and Atmospheric Administration (NOAA) Satellite Operations Facility, focused on Application Security – A Programmer's Perspective; Integrating Security into the Application Development Life Cycle; and Panel Discussion: Application Security Realities.

This year's annual two-day offsite meeting featured updates on the computer security activities of the Government Accountability Office (GAO), United States Computer Emergency Readiness Team (US-CERT), the Department of Homeland Security, and NIST. Technical sessions included briefings on Application Security, Basic Input/Output System (BIOS) Protection Guidelines, Federal Cybersecurity Workforce Initiatives, Information Security Continuous Monitoring, Cybersecurity Research and Development, Enterprise-wide Risk Management, Security Awareness and Training, and the U.S. Government Configuration Baseline (USGCB).

The number of members on the email list has grown steadily and provides a valuable resource for federal security program managers. To join, email your name, affiliation, address, phone number, title, and confirmation that you are a federal employee to sec-forum@nist.gov.

http://csrc.nist.gov/groups/SMA/forum/
Contacts:

Mr. Kevin Stine,	Ms. Peggy Himes,
Chair	Administration
(301) 975-4483	(301) 975-2489
kevin.stine@nist.gov	peggy.himes@nist.gov

Federal Information Systems Security Educators' Association (FISSEA)

The Federal Information Systems Security Educators' Association (FISSEA), founded in 1987, is an organization run by and for information systems security professionals to assist federal agencies in meeting their information systems security awareness, training, and education responsibilities. During the 2011 conference business meeting, it was announced that the NIST Computer Security Division will make a deeper commitment to FISSEA. The NIST plan includes a graceful transition to a NIST program supported by the current Executive Board. There will be direct and formal connections with the National Initiative for Cybersecurity Education (NICE). FISSEA strives to elevate the general level of information

systems security knowledge for the federal government and the federal workforce. FISSEA serves as a professional forum for the exchange of information and improvement of information systems security awareness, training, and education programs. It also seeks to assist the professional development of its members.

FISSEA membership is open to information systems security professionals, professional trainers and educators, and managers responsible for information systems security training programs in federal agencies, as well as contractors of these agencies and faculty members of accredited educational institutions who are involved in information security training and education. There are no membership fees to join FISSEA; all that is required is a willingness to share products, information, and experiences. Business is administered by a working group that meets monthly.

Each year an award is presented to a candidate selected as FISSEA Educator of the Year; this award honors distinguished accomplishments in information systems security training programs. Jim Wiggins of the Federal IT Security Institute was awarded the Educator of the Year for 2010 at the 2011 FISSEA Conference. Mark Wilson received the second FISSEA Life Member Award, for his leadership, outreach, and dedication to the FISSEA mission and many years of service as the NIST Liaison.

The annual FISSEA Security Awareness, Training and Education Contest consists of five categories from one of FISSEA's three key areas of Awareness, Training, and Education. The categories are: (1) awareness poster, (2) motivational item (aka: trinkets - pens, stress relief items, t-shirts, etc.), (3) awareness website, (4) awareness newsletter, and (5) role-based training and education. Winning entries for the security awareness contest are posted to the FISSEA website. The winners for the FY2011 contest were:

- Terri Cinnamon, Department of Veterans Affairs, had the winning motivational item;

- Maureen Moore, Food and Drug Administration, was selected for FDA's security newsletter as well as for their security website;

- David Kurtz of the Bureau of the Public Debt won the poster contest; and

- Defense Information Systems Agency (DISA), Science Applications International Corporation (SAIC), and Carney, Inc., were selected as the role-based training exercise winner.

FISSEA maintains a website, a list serve, and participates in a social networking site as a means of improving communication for its members. NIST assists FISSEA with its operations by providing staff support for several of its activities and by being FISSEA's host agency.

FISSEA membership in 2011 spanned federal agencies, industry, military, contractors, state governments, academia, the press, and foreign organizations to reach over 1,295 members in a total of ten countries. The 700 federal agency members represent 89 agencies from the executive and legislative branches of government.

On November 5, 2010, FISSEA hosted a workshop, *Connecting the DOTS - Harmonizing Current Cybersecurity Competency Efforts*, at NIH. Chris Kelsall, Director of the Cyber/IT Workforce, Department of the Navy, moderated a panel including Ernest McDuffie, lead for the National Initiative for Cybersecurity Education; Jacque Caldwell, lead Cybersecurity Competencies Efforts, U.S. Office of Personnel Management (OPM); Alan Carswell, Chair of the University of Maryland University College (UMUC) Cybersecurity Master's Program; and Dagne Fulcher, InfoSec Workforce Development Matrix Project. Attendees were able to obtain an overview of several cybersecurity workforce development efforts in order to enhance integration among past, current, and future endeavors. The workshop provided an open forum for discussion about how the efforts support, conflict, and/or overlap; attendees also shared viewpoints on concrete actions to support appropriate standardizing bodies.

The 2011 FISSEA conference returned to NIST on March 15-17, 2011, and the theme was *"Bridging to the Future - Emerging Trends in Cybersecurity."* The theme was chosen to reflect current projects, trends, and initiatives that will provide pathways to future solutions. Approximately 165 information systems security professionals and trainers attended, primarily from federal agencies, but also from academia and industry. Attendees received an update on the NICE activities, gained new techniques for developing and conducting training, as well as awareness and training ideas, resources, and contacts. Presenters represented NIST, the Department of Homeland Security (DHS), the Defense Intelligence Agency (DIA), the U.S. Department of State (DOS), the Department of Energy (DOE), the Department of Defense (DoD), the Department of Veterans Affairs (VA), the Internal Revenue Service (IRS), the National Aeronautics and Space Administration (NASA), the National Security Agency (NSA), the U.S. Office of Personnel Management (OPM), the Bureau of the Public Debt (BPD), and the Library of Congress. Presenters also represented private industry and academia. Attendees had an opportunity to visit 22 vendors on the second day. Another bonus of attending the FISSEA conference is social networking. The conference continues to be a valuable forum in which individuals from government, industry, and academia who are involved with information systems/cybersecurity workforce development - awareness, training, education, certification, and professionalization - may learn of ongoing and planned training and education programs and initiatives.

FISSEA has coordinated a Working Group to facilitate the development of an updated draft of SP 800-16, *Information Technology Security Training Requirements: A Role- and Performance-Based Model*. This effort reflects a significant commitment from FISSEA to advance Information Technology Awareness, Training, and Education.

The 2012 FISSEA conference is being planned for March 27-29, 2012 at NIST.

---

http://csrc.nist.gov/fissea
fisseamembership@nist.gov
Contacts:

Ms. Patricia Toth	Ms. Peggy Himes
(301) 975-5140	(301) 975-2489
patricia.toth@nist.gov	peggy.himes@nist.gov

Information Security and Privacy Advisory Board (ISPAB)

The Information Security and Privacy Advisory Board (ISPAB) is a federal advisory committee. It brings together senior professionals from industry, government, and academia to advise NIST, the Office of Management and Budget (OMB), the Secretary of Commerce, and appropriate committees of the U.S. Congress about information security and privacy issues pertaining to unclassified federal government information systems.

The ISPAB was originally created by the Computer Security Act of 1987 (P.L. 100-35) as the Computer System Security and Privacy Advisory Board, and amended by Public Law 107-347, Title III of the E-Government Act of 2002, the Federal Information Security Management Act (FISMA) of 2002. The Board's name was changed as a result of FISMA, and its mandate was amended. The scope and objectives of the Board are to—

- Identify emerging managerial, technical, administrative, and physical safeguard issues relative to information security and privacy;

- Advise NIST, the Secretary of Commerce, and the Director of OMB on information security and privacy issues pertaining to federal government information systems, including thorough review of proposed standards and guidelines developed by NIST; and

- Annually report the Board's findings to the Secretary of Commerce, the Director of OMB, the Director of the National Security Agency, and the appropriate committees of the Congress.

The charter (http://csrc.nist.gov/groups/SMA/ispab/documents/ispab_charter-2012-2014.pdf) defines that the Board's membership should consist of 12 members and a Chairperson. The term of office for each board member is four years. The Director of NIST approves membership appointments and appoints the Chairperson. During FY2011, the ISPAB Board members were:

- Daniel Chenok (Chair), IBM Center for The Business of Government;
- Julie Boughn, Center for Medicare and Medicaid Innovation, Department of Human Health and Services, Centers for Medicare & Medicaid Services (DHHS/CMS);
- Brian Gouker, National Security Agency (NSA) - U.S. Army War College;
- Joseph Guirreri, P E Systems, Inc.;
- Edward Roback, U.S. Department of Treasury;
- Phyllis Schneck, McAfee, Inc.;
- Gale Stone, Social Security Administration;
- Matthew Thomlinson, Microsoft; and
- Peter Weinberger, Google, Inc.

The following Board members were nominated to the ISPAB Board after September 30, 2011:

- Kevin Fu, University of Massachusetts Amherst;
- Greg Garcia, Bank of America; and
- Toby Levin, Retired

This advisory board of experienced, dynamic, and knowledgeable professionals provides NIST and the federal government with a rich, varied pool of people conversant with an extraordinary range of topics.

Front row (L-R): Megan St. Clair, Matt Scholl, Phyllis Schneck, Dan Chenok, Annie Sokol, Kevin Fu, Brian Gouker, Gale Stone
Back row (L-R): Peter Weinberger, Matt Thomlinson, Joe Guirreri, Toby Levin, Greg Garcia, Ed Roback

The Board's membership draws from experience at all levels of information security and privacy work. The members' careers cover government, industry, and academia. Members have worked in the executive and legislative branches of the federal government, civil service, senior executive service, the military, some of the largest corporations worldwide, small and medium-size businesses, and some of the top universities in the nation. The members' experience, likewise, covers a broad spectrum of activities including many different engineering disciplines, computer programming, systems analysis, mathematics, management, information technology auditing, privacy, and law. Members also have an extensive history of professional publications, and professional journalism. Members have worked (and in many cases, continue to work) on the development and evolution of some of the most important pieces of information security and privacy legislation in the federal government, including the Privacy Act of 1974, the Computer Security Act of 1987, the E-Government Act (including FISMA), and other e-government services and initiatives.

In FY2011, the board lost three longtime members: Lynn McNulty, Alexander L. Popowycz, and Fred Schneider. In the same period, the Board is pleased to welcome two new members, Julie Boughn and Edward Roback. They all bring great depth to a field that has an exceptional rate of change.

The Board usually meets three times per year and meetings are open to the public. NIST provides the Board with its Secretariat. The Board has received numerous briefings from federal and private sector representatives on a wide range of privacy and security topics in the past year. Areas of interest that the Board followed in FY2011 were:

- Cloud Computing Security and Privacy;
- Cybersecurity Legislation;
- Health IT, Medical Devices in relation to cybersecurity and privacy;
- Access to Classified Information and Cybersecurity;
- Cybersecurity Workforce for Industry and Government with focus on SCADA (supervisory control and data acquisition) Systems and Security and Reverse Engineering;
- Usability and Security;
- Domain Name System Security (DNSSec);
- Legislature and Security;
- Direct Hiring and Cybersecurity education;
- International Standards and Cybersecurity;
- National Information Assurance Partnership (NIAP) Testing and Assurance; and
- Continued Critical Infrastructure Protection (CIP) Report and Industrial Control Systems Security;

- Federal Initiatives such as:
  - National Initiative for Cybersecurity Education (NICE);
  - National Strategy for Trusted Identities in Cyberspace (NSTIC);
  - Security Content Automation Protocol (SCAP) – Security Automation and Vulnerability Management;
  - National Vulnerability Database (NVD);
  - Federal Risk and Authorization Management Pilot program (FedRAMP);
  - United States Computer Emergency Readiness Team (US-CERT);
  - Homeland Security Presidential Directive (HSPD) 12;
  - National Cybersecurity and Communications Integration Center (NCCIC) and Cyber Storm;
  - Continuous Monitoring;
  - FISMA; and
  - NIST's outreach, research, and strategies.

http://csrc.nist.gov/ispab/
Contact:
  Ms. Annie Sokol
  (301) 975-2006
  annie.sokol@nist.gov

Small and Medium-Sized Business (SMB) Outreach

What do business invoices have in common with email? If both are done on the same computer, the business owner may want to think more about computer security information – payroll records, proprietary information, client or employee data – as essential to a business's success. A computer failure or system breach could cost a business anything from its reputation to damages and recovery costs. The small business owner who recognizes the threat of computer crime and takes steps to deter inappropriate activities is less likely to become a victim.

The vulnerability of any one small business may not seem significant to many people, other than the owner and employees of that business. However, over 20 million U.S. businesses, comprising more than 95 percent of all U.S. businesses, are small and medium-size businesses (SMBs) of 500 employees or less (http://www.sba.gov/sites/default/files/files/us10.pdf). Therefore, a vulnerability common to a large percentage of SMBs could pose a threat to the nation's information infrastructure and economic base. SMBs frequently cannot justify the employment

of an extensive security program or a full-time expert. Nonetheless, they confront serious security challenges.

The difficulty for these businesses is to identify security mechanisms and training that are practical and cost-effective. Such businesses also need to become more educated in terms of security so that limited resources are well applied to meet the most relevant and serious threats. To address this need, NIST, the Small Business Administration (SBA), and the Federal Bureau of Investigation (FBI) are cosponsoring a series of training workshops on computer security for small businesses. The purpose of the meetings is to provide an overview of information security threats, vulnerabilities, and corresponding protective tools and techniques, with a special emphasis on providing useful information that small business personnel can apply directly.

In FY2011, six SMB outreach workshops were provided in five cities: Knoxville, Tennessee; Fort Lauderdale, Florida; Ruidoso, New Mexico; Orlando, Florida; and Gaithersburg, Maryland. In September, the last SMB outreach workshop was presented at the NICE (National Initiative for Cybersecurity Education) Annual Workshop in Gaithersburg, Maryland.

In collaboration with the SBA and the FBI, planning is under way to identify locations for small business information security workshops in FY2012.

http://sbc.nist.gov
Contact:
  Mr. Richard Kissel
  (301) 975-5017
  richard.kissel@nist.gov

Health Information Technology Security

Health information technology (HIT) makes it possible for healthcare providers to better manage patient care through secure use and sharing of health information, leading to improvements in healthcare quality, reduced medical errors, increased efficiencies in care delivery and administration, and improved population health. Central to reaching these goals is the assurance of the confidentiality, integrity, and availability of health information. The CSD works actively with government, industry, academia, and others to provide security tools, technologies, and methodologies that provide for the security and privacy of health information.

In FY2011, NIST initiated development of a HIT security self-assessment toolkit which is intended to help organizations better understand the requirements of the Health Insurance Portability and Accountability Act (HIPAA) Security Rule, implement those requirements, and assess those implementations in their operational environment. This project also enables NIST to leverage security automation specifications within the context of the healthcare use case. NIST also began development of baseline security configurations for common operating systems used in electronic health record (EHR) implementations to enable greater automation of HIT and HIPAA Security Rule technical safeguards.

NIST also continued its HIT security outreach efforts in FY2011. NIST and the Department of Health and Human Services' (DHHS) Office for Civil Rights (OCR) cohosted the fourth annual HIPAA Security Rule conference, *"Safeguarding Health Information: Building Assurance through HIPAA Security,"* in May 2011 at the Ronald Reagan Building and International Trade Center in Washington, D.C. Nearly 400 in-person and webcast attendees from federal, state, and local governments, academia, HIPAA-covered entities and business associates, industry groups, and vendors heard from and interacted with healthcare, security, and privacy experts on technologies and methodologies for safeguarding health information and for implementing the requirements of the HIPAA Security Rule. Presentations covered a variety of topics including updates on OCR's health information privacy and security regulations and enforcement activities; applicability of the National Strategy for Trusted Identities in Cyberspace (NSTIC) to the healthcare sector; insider threat trends and safeguards; medical device security market trends and practical security strategies; mobile computing trends in healthcare; security automation applications; risk analysis in a multisite practice setting; and securing health information in the Cloud.

In FY2012, NIST plans to release a HIPAA Security self-assessment toolkit and baseline security configuration automation content. NIST also plans to issue a draft revision to Special Publication (SP) 800-66, *An Introductory Resource Guide for Implementing the HIPAA Security Rule.* As part of its continued outreach efforts, NIST also plans to host the fifth annual *"Safeguarding Health Information"* conference.

http://www.nist.gov/healthcare/security/index.cfm

Contacts:

Mr. Kevin Stine
(301) 975-4483
kevin.stine@nist.gov

Mr. Matthew Scholl
(301) 975-2941
matthew.scholl@nist.gov

National Initiative for Cybersecurity Education (NICE)

NIST was designated as the lead for the National Initiative for Cybersecurity Education (NICE) in a March 2010 recommendation of the Information and Communications Infrastructure – Interagency Policy Committee (ICI-IPC). This recommendation was based on chapter two of the May 2009 Cyberspace Policy Review titled "Building Capacity for a Digital Nation" and is responsive to President Obama's declaration that the "cyber threat is one of the most serious economic and national security challenges we face as a nation" and that "America's economic prosperity in the 21st century will depend on cybersecurity."

The goal of NICE is to enhance the overall cybersecurity posture of the United States by accelerating the availability of educational and training resources designed to improve the cyber behavior, skills, and knowledge of every segment of the population, enabling a safer cyberspace for all. NICE will address this challenging goal by:

- Raising awareness among the American public about the risks of online activities;

- Broadening the pool of skilled workers capable of supporting a cyber-secure nation; and

- Developing and maintaining an unrivaled, globally competitive cybersecurity workforce.

This initiative comprises four component areas: National Cybersecurity Awareness; Formal Cybersecurity Education; Cybersecurity Workforce Structure; and Cybersecurity Workforce Training and Professional Development. As the designated initiative lead, NIST promotes the coordination of existing and future activities in cybersecurity education, training, and awareness to enhance and multiply their effectiveness.

In FY2011, NIST issued the draft NICE Strategic Plan, "Building a Digital Nation." This plan was developed from separate drafts that expressed the views of the four component areas into a comprehensive document that will be submitted for Cyber IPC approval.

NIST organized and hosted the second annual NICE Workshop, *"Shaping the Future of Cybersecurity Education,"* held on September 20-22, 2011. The workshop served as a forum for the community to openly discuss progress, solutions, challenges, and proposals relating to the goals of the NICE program. Over 500 attendees from academia, government, and industry joined in the workshop, either in person or virtually through webinars/webcasts. The participation of universities, community colleges, high schools, and other training associations, including international groups from Canada, Japan, Brazil and Italy, exceeded expectations. As part of its outreach role, the NIST NICE Leadership Team (NNLT) members also attended more than 100 events, symposia, forums, competitions, educational outreach meetings, and workshops to promote the initiative.

In FY2012, NIST plans to finalize the NICE Strategic Plan, communications plan, and component-specific implementation plans and baseline studies. NIST will also continue to improve the NICE website and host the third annual NICE workshop.

http://www.nist.gov/nice/
Contacts:

Dr. Ernest McDuffie,
NICE Project Lead
(301) 975-8897
ernest.mcduffie@nist.gov

Mr. Bill Newhouse
(301) 975-2869
william.newhouse@nist.gov

Ms. Magdalena Benitez
(301) 975-6182
mbenitez@nist.gov

Ms. Pat Toth
(301) 975-5140
ptoth@nist.gov

Ms. Richard Kissel
(301) 975-5017
richard.kissel@nist.gov

Ms. Celia Paulsen
(301) 975-5981
celia.paulsen@nist.gov

Smart Grid Cyber Security

The major elements of the Smart Grid are the information technology, the industrial control systems, and the communications infrastructure used to send command information across the electric grid, from generation to distribution systems, and to exchange usage and billing information between utilities and their customers. Key to the successful deployment of the Smart Grid infrastructure is the development of the cybersecurity strategy for the Smart Grid. In fact, cybersecurity needs to be designed into the deploying systems that support Smart Grid, and added into existing systems. The electric grid is critical to the economic and physical well-being of the nation, and emerging cyber threats targeting power systems highlight the need to integrate advanced security to protect critical assets.

NIST established the Smart Grid Interoperability Panel (SGIP) Cyber Security Working Group (CSWG) in support of the Energy Independence and Security Act of 2007 to address the cross-cutting issue of cybersecurity. The CSWG has more than 650 participants worldwide from the private sector (including utilities, vendors, and service providers), academia, regulatory organizations, state and local government, and U.S. federal agencies. Membership in the CSWG is free and is open to all. Many members participate from around the world by monitoring the minutes and email conversations of the subgroups.

The CSWG membership collaborated to deliver the NIST Interagency Report (NISTIR) 7628, *Guidelines for Smart Grid Cyber Security*, in August 2010. Since then the group has focused on specific topics, such as risk management processes, key management in the Smart Grid, the Smart Grid security architecture, security testing and certification, Advanced Metering Infrastructure (AMI) security, and privacy in the Smart Grid. In addition, the group is conducting security reviews of many Smart Grid-related standards.

To complete the work, there are seven subgroups that focus on specific topics. During the development of NISTIR 7628, the subgroups performed detailed technical analysis on an array of security-related topics, and then documented the research, issues, and guidance in specific sections. The approach taken by all subgroups is an open and collaborative process in which any CSWG member is welcome to participate and contribute.

The CSWG creates and disbands subgroups as needed to meet present needs. Since the NISTIR 7628 v1.0 publication, some of the CSWG subgroups merged, while others are regrouping as they determine their next set of tasks. The CSWG currently consists of the following subgroups:

- The **Advanced Metering Infrastructure (AMI) Security subgroup** plans to create a set of AMI security requirements.

- The **Architecture subgroup** focuses on the enhancement of the logical security architecture for the Smart Grid. This group's work is used as input to the SGIP Architecture Committee.

- The **Design Principles subgroup** continues the work of identifying bottom-up problems and design considerations developed by the former Bottom-up, Vulnerability, and Cryptography and Key Management subgroups.

- The **High-Level Requirements subgroup** addresses the procedural and technical security requirements of the Smart Grid to be addressed by stakeholders in Smart Grid security. To create the initial set of security requirements in NISTIR 7628 v1.0, this subgroup adapted industry-accepted security source documents for the Smart Grid.

- The **Privacy subgroup** continues to investigate privacy concerns between utilities, consumers, and non-utility third parties.

- The **Standards subgroup** assesses standards and other documents with respect to the cybersecurity and privacy requirements from NISTIR 7628. These assessments are performed on the standards contained in the SP 1108, *Framework and Roadmap for Smart Grid Interoperability Standards,* or in support of the Priority Action Plans (PAPs).

- The **Testing and Certification subgroup** establishes guidance and methodologies for cybersecurity testing of Smart Grid systems, subsystems, and components.

Future work includes working with the SGIP — the Committees, the Domain Expert Working Groups, and the Priority Action Plans — to integrate cybersecurity into their work efforts. Collaboration will continue with the Department of Energy and the North American Electric Reliability Corporation to produce a cybersecurity risk management process document for the electricity sector. Reviewing and updating NISTIR 7628, if needed, will occur in early 2012. Developing a virtual test environment for the National Electrical Manufacturers Association's AMI upgradeability standard and creating an assessment guide for assessing the high-level cybersecurity requirements contained in NISTIR 7628 are also slated for the next year.

http://collaborate.nist.gov/twiki-sggrid/bin/view/SmartGrid/

Contacts:

Ms. Marianne Swanson	Ms. Tanya Brewer
(301) 975-3293	(301) 975-4534
marianne.swanson@nist.gov	tbrewer@nist.gov

ICT Supply Chain Risk Management

Federal agency information systems and networks are increasingly at risk of both intentional and unintentional supply chain compromise due to the growing sophistication of information and communications technologies (ICT) and the growing speed and scale of a complex, distributed global supply chain. Federal agencies currently have neither a consistent nor comprehensive way of understanding the often opaque processes and practices used to create and deliver hardware and software products and services that are contracted out, especially beyond the prime contractor. This lack of understanding, visibility, and control increases the risk of exploitation through a variety of means including counterfeit materials, malicious software, or untrustworthy products, and makes it increasingly difficult for federal agencies to understand their exposure and manage the associated supply chain risks.

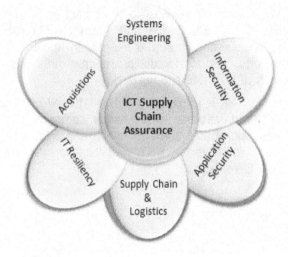

Figure Above: Components and Contributing Disciplines of ICT SCRM

In 2011, NIST continued to develop NISTIR 7622, *Notional Supply Chain Risk Management Practices for Federal Information Systems.* This document discusses the following topics:

- Determining which procurements should consider supply chain risk;

- Describing the key roles and responsibilities within the organization as they relate to supply chain risk management;

- Working with the procurement office, legal counsel, information system security personnel, and other appropriate agency stakeholders to help mitigate supply chain risk through the careful selection of security and supply chain contractual requirements; and

- Mitigating supply chain risk by augmenting the baseline of security controls defined for the information system through additional practices contained in the document.

NIST also issued a grant to the University of Maryland, Robert H. Smith School of Business, Supply Chain Management Center, to research and inventory existing supply chain risk management (SCRM) initiatives in industry and government and develop an integrative architecture that can understand the contribution and reach of each initiative in the context of an end-to-end SCRM process model. Current ICT SCRM practices are functionally fragmented and vertically stove-piped. This research is expected to assist NIST's development of SCRM best practices by helping close existing knowledge and data gaps.

In 2012, NIST will continue to work with government, industry, academia, and others to identify and evaluate technologies, tools, techniques, best practices, and standards useful in securing the ICT supply chain. NIST will use that information to develop SCRM tools and a Special Publication on ICT SCRM Best Practices for federal information systems.

---

http://scrm.nist.gov/
Contact:
   Mr. Jon Boyens
   (301) 975-5549
   jon.boyens@nist.gov

Cryptographic Validation Program

Cryptographic Validation Programs and Laboratory Accreditation

The Cryptographic Algorithm Validation Program (CAVP) and the Cryptographic Module Validation Program (CMVP) were developed by NIST to support the needs of the user community for strong, independently tested, and commercially available cryptographic algorithms and modules. Through these programs, NIST works with private and governmental sectors and the cryptographic community to achieve security, interoperability, and assurance of correct implementation. The goal of these programs is to promote the use of validated algorithms, modules, and products and to provide federal agencies with a security metric to use in procuring cryptographic modules. The

testing carried out by accredited laboratories and the validations performed by these two programs provide this metric. Federal agencies, industry, and the public can choose cryptographic modules and/or products containing cryptographic modules from the CMVP Validated Modules List and have confidence in the claimed level of security and assurance of correct implementation.

Cryptographic algorithm and cryptographic module testing and validation are based on underlying published standards and guidance that are developed within the Computer Security Division (CSD) in collaboration with many other organizations. As federal agencies are required to use validated cryptographic modules for the protection of sensitive nonclassified information, the validated modules and the validated algorithms that the modules contain represent the culmination and delivery of the division's cryptography-based work to the end user.

The CAVP and the CMVP are separate, collaborative programs based on a partnership between NIST's CSD and the Communication Security Establishment Canada (CSEC). The programs provide federal agencies — in the United States and Canada — confidence that a validated cryptographic algorithm has been implemented correctly and that a validated cryptographic module meets a claimed level of security assurance. The CAVP and the CMVP validate algorithms and modules used in a wide variety of products, including secure Internet browsers, secure radios, smart cards, space-based communications, munitions, security tokens, storage devices, and products supporting Public Key Infrastructure (PKI) and electronic commerce. A module may be a stand-alone product, such

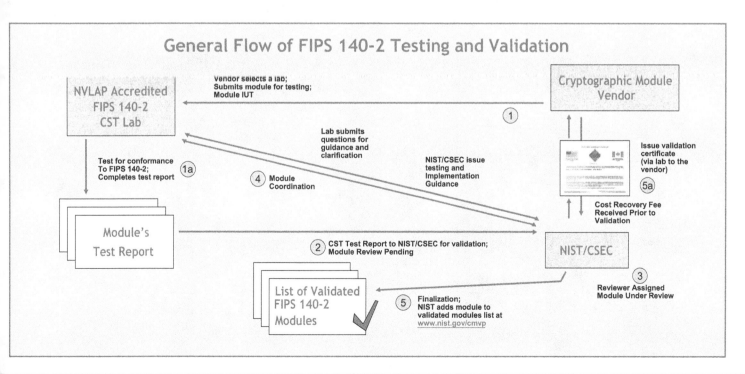

General Flow of FIPS 140-2 Testing and Validation

as a virtual private network (VPN), smart card or toolkit, or one module may be used in several products; as a result, a small number of modules may be incorporated within hundreds of products. Likewise, the CAVP validates cryptographic algorithms that may be integrated in one or more cryptographic modules.

The two validation programs (the CAVP and CMVP) provide documented methodologies for conformance testing through defined sets of security requirements. Security requirements for the CAVP are found in the individual validation system documents containing the validation test suites that are required to assure that the algorithm has been implemented correctly. The validation system documents are designed for each FIPS-approved and NIST-recommended cryptographic algorithm. Security requirements for the CMVP are found in FIPS 140-2, *Security Requirements for Cryptographic Modules,* and the associated test metrics and methods in Derived Test Requirements for FIPS 140-2. Annexes to FIPS 140-2 reference the underlying cryptographic algorithm standards or methods. Federal agencies are required to use modules that were validated as conforming to the provisions of FIPS 140-2. The CMVP developed Derived Test Requirements associated with FIPS 140-2 to define the security requirements and the test metrics and methods to ensure repeatability of tests and equivalency in results across the testing laboratories.

The CMVP reviews the cryptographic modules validation requests and, as a byproduct of the review, is attentive to emerging and/or changing technologies and the evolution of operating environments and complex systems during the module validation review activities. Likewise, the CAVP reviews the cryptographic algorithm validation requests submitted by the accredited laboratories. With these insights, the CAVP and CMVP can perform research and development of new test metrics and methods as they evolve. Based on this research, the CAVP and CMVP publish implementation guidance to assist vendors, testing laboratories, and the user community in the latest programmatic and technical guidance. This guidance provides clarity, consistency of interpretation, and insight for successful conformance testing, validation, and revalidation.

The unique position of the validation programs gives them the opportunity to acquire insight during the validation review activities and results in practical, timely, and up-to-date guidance that is needed by the testing laboratories and vendors to move their modules and products out to the user community in a timely and cost-effective manner and with the assurance of third-party conformance testing. This knowledge and insight provide a foundation for future standards development.

The CAVP and the CMVP have stimulated improved quality and security assurance of cryptographic modules. The latest set of statistics, which are collected quarterly from each of the testing laboratories, show that 8 percent of the cryptographic algorithms and 61 percent of the cryptographic modules brought in for voluntary testing had security flaws that were corrected during testing. Without this program, the federal government would have had less than a 50 percent chance of buying correctly implemented cryptography. To date, over 1,615 cryptographic module validation certificates have been issued, representing over 3,500 modules that were validated by the CMVP. These modules have been developed by more than 335 domestic and international vendors.

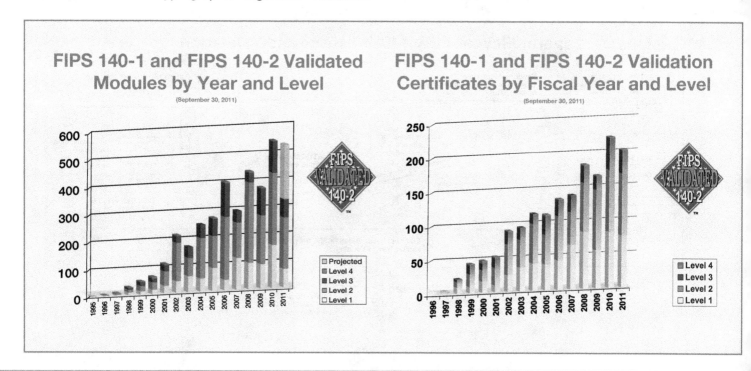

CAVP Validation Status By FYs

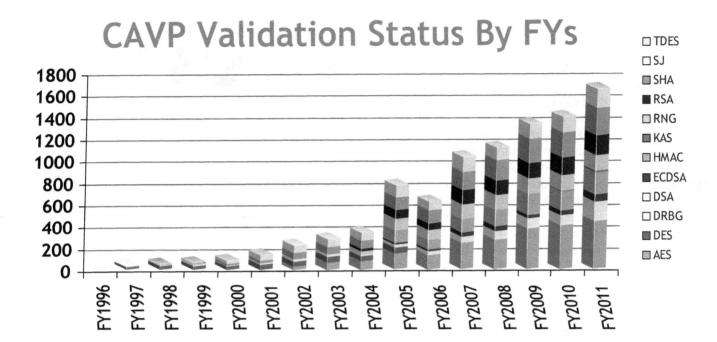

CAVP Validated Implementation Actual Numbers

Updated As Thursday, October 06, 2011

FiscalYear	AES	DES	DSA	DRBG	ECDSA	HMAC	KAS	RNG	RSA	SHA	SJ	TDES	Total
FY1996	0	2	0	0	0	0	0	0	0	0	0	0	2
FY1997	0	11	6	0	0	0	0	0	0	7	2	0	26
FY1998	0	27	9	0	0	0	0	0	0	6	0	0	42
FY1999	0	30	14	0	0	0	0	0	0	12	1	0	57
FY2000	0	29	7	0	0	0	0	0	0	12	1	28	77
FY2001	0	41	15	0	0	0	0	0	0	28	0	51	135
FY2002	30	44	21	0	0	0	0	0	0	59	6	58	218
FY2003	66	49	24	0	0	0	0	0	0	63	3	73	278
FY2004	82	41	17	0	0	0	0	28	22	77	0	70	337
FY2005	145	54	31	0	14	115	0	108	80	122	2	102	773
FY2006	131	3	33	0	19	87	0	91	63	120	1	83	631
FY2007	238	0	63	0	35	127	0	137	130	171	1	136	1038
FY2008	271	0	77	4	41	158	0	137	129	191	0	122	1130
FY2009	373	0	71	23	33	193	3	142	143	224	1	138	1344
FY2010	399	0	70	31	39	179	6	150	155	239	0	142	1410
FY2011	440	0	102	79	68	201	17	148	183	255	0	176	1669
Total	2175	331	560	137	249	1060	26	941	905	1586	18	1179	9167

The CAVP issued 1,669 algorithm validations and the CMVP issued 202 module validation certificates in FY2011. The number of algorithms and modules submitted for validation continues to grow, representing significant growth in the number of validated products expected to be available in the future.

http://csrc.nist.gov/groups/STM
Contacts:

CMVP Contact:
Mr. Randall J. Easter
(301) 975-4641
randall.easter@nist.gov

CAVP Contact:
Ms. Sharon Keller
(301) 975-2910
sharon.keller@nist.gov

Automated Security Testing and Test Suite Development

Federal Information Processing Standards (FIPS) and Special Publications (SPs) define the FIPS-recommended and NIST-approved cryptographic algorithms recognized by the federal government. The detailed specifications of the cryptographic algorithms and how they are to be implemented are contained within these documents. Automated security testing of these cryptographic algorithms provides a uniform way to assure that the cryptographic algorithm implementation adheres to the detailed specifications. Validation test suites are designed and developed by the CAVP. These tests exercise the mathematical formulas detailed in the algorithm to assure that the detailed specifications are implemented correctly and completely. If the implementer deviates from these instructions or excludes any part of the instructions, the validation test will fail, indicating that the algorithm implementation does not function properly or is incomplete.

There are several types of validation tests, all designed to satisfy the testing requirements of the cryptographic algorithms and their specifications. These include, but are not limited to, Known Answer Tests, Monte Carlo Tests, and Multi-Block Message Tests. The Known Answer Tests are designed to test the conformance of the implementation under test (IUT) to the various specifications in the reference. This involves testing the components of the algorithm to assure that they are implemented correctly. The Monte Carlo Test is designed to exercise the entire IUT. This test is designed to detect the presence of implementation flaws that are not detected with the controlled input of the Known Answer Tests. The types of implementation flaws detected by this validation test include pointer problems, insufficient allocation of space, improper error handling, and incorrect behavior of the IUT. The Multi-Block Message Test (MMT) is designed to test the ability of the implementation to process multi-block messages, which require the chaining of information from one block to the next.

Automated security testing and test suite development are integral components of the CAVP. The CAVP encompasses validation testing for FIPS-approved and NIST-recommended cryptographic algorithms. Cryptographic algorithm validation is a prerequisite to the CMVP. The testing of cryptographic algorithm implementations is performed by independent third-party laboratories that are accredited as Cryptographic and Security Testing (CST) laboratories by the NIST National Voluntary Laboratory Accreditation Program (NVLAP). The CAVP develops and maintains a Cryptographic Algorithm Validation System (CAVS) tool that automates the cryptographic algorithm validation testing.

The CAVS currently has algorithm validation testing for the following cryptographic algorithms:

Cryptographic Algorithm/Component	Special Publication or FIPS
Triple Data Encryption Standard (TDES)	SP 800-67, *Recommendation for the Triple Data Encryption Algorithm (TDEA) Block Cipher*, and SP 800-38A, *Recommendation for Block Cipher Modes of Operation - Methods and Techniques*
Advanced Encryption Standard (AES)	FIPS 197, *Advanced Encryption Standard*, and SP 800-38A
Digital Signature Standard (DSS)	FIPS 186-2, *Digital Signature Standard (DSS,)* with change notice 1, dated October 5, 2001
	FIPS 186-3, *Digital Signature Standard (DSS)*, dated June 2009
Elliptic Curve Digital Signature Algorithm (ECDSA)	FIPS 186-2, *Digital Signature Standard (DSS,)* with change notice 1, dated October 5, 2001 and ANSI X9.62
	FIPS 186-3, *Digital Signature Standard (DSS)*, dated June 2009 and ANSI X9.62
RSA algorithm	ANSI X9.31 and Public Key Cryptography Standards (PKCS) #1 v2.1: RSA Cryptography Standard-2002
	FIPS 186-3, *Digital Signature Standard (DSS)*, dated June 2009 and ANSI X9.31 and Public Key Cryptography Standards (PKCS) #1 v2.1: RSA Cryptography Standard-2002
Hashing algorithms SHA-1, SHA-224, SHA-256, SHA-384, and SHA-512	FIPS 180-3, *Secure Hash Standard (SHS)*, dated October 2008
Random number generator (RNG) algorithms	FIPS 186-2 Appendix 3.1 and 3.2; ANSI X9.62 Appendix A.4
Deterministic Random Bit Generators (DRBG)	SP 800-90, *Recommendation for Random Number Generation Using Deterministic Random Bit Generators*
Keyed-Hash Message Authentication Code (HMAC)	FIPS 198, *The Keyed-Hash Message Authentication Code (HMAC)*
Counter with Cipher Block Chaining-Message Authentication Code (CCM) mode	SP 800-38C, *Recommendation for Block Cipher Modes of Operation: the CCM Mode for Authentication and Confidentiality*

Cipher-based Message Authentication Code (CMAC) Mode for Authentication	SP 800-38B, *Recommendation for Block Cipher Modes of Operation: The CMAC Mode for Authentication*
Galois/Counter Mode (GCM) GMAC Mode of Operation	SP 800-38D, *Recommendation for Block Cipher Modes of Operation: Galois/Counter Mode (GCM) and GMAC*, dated November 2007
XTS Mode of Operation	SP800-38E, *Recommendation for Block Cipher Modes of Operation: The XTS-AES Mode for Confidentiality on Block-Oriented Storage Devices*, dated January 2010
Key Agreement Schemes and Key Confirmation	SP 800-56A, *Recommendation for Pair-Wise Key Establishment Schemes Using Discrete Logarithm Cryptography*, dated March 2007
All of SP 800-56A except KDF	SP 800-56A All sections except Section 5.8 *Key Derivation Functions for Key Agreement Schemes*
SP 800-56A Section 5.7.1.2 ECC CDH function	SP 800-56A Section 5.7.1.2 *Elliptic Curve Cryptography Cofactor Diffie-Hellman (ECC CDH) Primitive Testing*

In FY2012, the CAVP expects to augment the CAVS tool to provide algorithm validation testing for:

- SP 800-108, *Recommendation for Key Derivation Using Pseudorandom Functions*, dated November 2008;
- SP 800-135, *Recommendation for Existing Application-Specific Key Derivation Functions*, dated December 2010; and
- SP 800-56B, *Recommendation for Pair-Wise Key Establishment Schemes Using Integer Factorization Cryptography*, dated August 2009.

http://csrc.nist.gov/groups/STM/cavp
Contact:
Ms. Sharon Keller
(301) 975-2910
sharon.keller@nist.gov

ISO Standardization of Security Requirements for Cryptographic Modules

CSD has contributed to the activities of the International Organization for Standardization/International Electrotechnical Commission (ISO/IEC), which issued ISO/IEC 19790, *Security Requirements for Cryptographic Modules*, on March 1, 2006, and ISO/IEC 24759, *Test Requirements for Cryptographic Modules*, on July 1, 2008. These efforts bring consistent testing of cryptographic modules to the global community.

ISO/IEC JTC 1/SC 27 WG 3 has progressed on the revision of ISO/IEC 19790 and the revision of ISO/IEC 24759 for which Randall J. Easter of CSD is the editor. In June 2011, revision 19790 moved to Committee Draft (CD) status and circulated for national body comment. It is expected that the revision of 19790 will be published in FY2012. The first working draft of 24759 was completed in June 2011 and circulated for national body comment.

Work is progressing on a new Technical Report document, ISO/IEC 30104 "*Physical Security Attacks, Mitigation Techniques and Security Requirements,*" for which Randall J. Easter of CSD is the editor. The second working draft of 30104 was completed in June 2011 and circulated for national body comment.

National body comments for the above three documents will be addressed at the 43rd SC 27 WG 3 meeting to be held in Nairobi, Kenya, in October 2011.

A new work item was proposed at the 42rd SC 27 WG 3 meeting, which was held in April 2011, to address *Testing Methods for the Mitigation of Non-invasive Attack Classes Against Cryptographic Modules*. It was proposed that this new document will be referenced by ISO/IEC rev19790 to define the test metrics to support the testing of cryptographic modules that have implemented non-invasive mitigation techniques. It is expected to be approved as a new work item at the 43rd SC 27 WG 3 with Randall J. Easter of CSD appointed as editor.

http://csrc.nist.gov/groups/STM/cmvp/
Contact:
Mr. Randall J. Easter
(301) 975-4641
randall.easter@nist.gov

Cryptographic Technology Group

Strategic Goal

Develop and improve mechanisms to protect the integrity, confidentiality, and authenticity of federal agency information by developing security mechanisms, standards, testing methods, and supporting infrastructure requirements and procedures.

Overview

The Cryptographic Technology Group's work in cryptographic mechanisms addresses topics such as hash algorithms, symmetric and asymmetric cryptographic techniques, key management and authentication. The Group's work in hardware roots of trust is designed to extend the value of these mechanisms to support reliable device authentication and establish new bases for system measurement. In cryptographic protocols, focus areas include Internet security services, security applications, identity management, and smart tokens. The Group continued to make an impact in the field of cryptography both within and outside the federal government by collaborating with national and international agencies, academic and research organizations, and standards bodies to develop interoperable security standards and guidelines.

Federal agency collaborators include the National Security Agency (NSA), the National Telecommunications and Information Administration (NTIA), the General Services Administration (GSA), the Election Assistance Commission (EAC) and the Federal Voting Assistance Program (FVAP). International agencies include the Communications Security Establishment of Canada, and Australia's Defense Signals Agency and Centrelink. National and international standards bodies include the American Standards Committee (ASC) X9 (financial industry standards), the International Organization for Standardization (ISO), the Institute of Electrical and Electronics Engineers (IEEE), the Internet Engineering Task Force (IETF), and the Trusted Computing Group (TCG). Industry collaborators include Intel, Dell, Hewlett Packard, VeriSign, Certicom, Entrust Technologies, Microsoft, Orion Security, RSA Security, Voltage Security, Verifone, Juniper, and Cisco. Academic collaborators include Katholieke Universiteit Leuven, George Mason University, Danmarks Tekniske Universitet, George Washington University, SDU Odense, UC Davis, Malaga University, and Yale University. Academic and research organizations include the International Association for Cryptologic Research (IACR), the European Network of Excellence in Cryptology (ECRYPT) II and the Japanese Cryptography Research and Evaluation Committees (CRYPTREC).

Strong cryptography, developed in part by the Group, can be used to improve the security of information systems and the information they process. Users can then take advantage of the availability of secure applications in the marketplace that is made possible by the appropriate use of standardized high quality cryptography. This work also supports the NIST's Personal Identity Verification (PIV) project in response to the Homeland Security Presidential Directive 12 (HSPD-12); for further details see *Personal Identity Verification* (PIV) section under the Systems and Emerging Technologies Security Research Group.

Cryptographic Standards Toolkit

Hash Algorithms and the Secure Hash Standard (SHA)-3 Competition

The Cryptographic Technology Group is responsible for the maintenance and development of the *Secure Hash Standard* specified in Federal Information Processing Standard (FIPS) 180-3. A hash algorithm processes a message, which can be very large, and produces a condensed representation, called the message digest. A cryptographic hash algorithm is a fundamental component of many cryptographic functions, such as digital signature algorithms, key derivation functions, keyed-hash message authentication codes, or random number generators. Cryptographic hash algorithms are frequently used in Internet protocols or in other security applications.

In 2005, researchers developed an attack that threatens the security of the NIST-approved government hash algorithm standard, SHA-1. Since then, researchers at NIST and elsewhere have also discovered several generic limitations in the basic Merkle-Damgard construct that is used in SHA-1 and most other existing hash algorithms. To address these vulnerabilities, NIST opened a public competition in November 2007 to develop a new cryptographic hash algorithm, which will be called "SHA-3" and will augment the hash algorithms currently specified in FIPS 180-3.

CSD selected 51 first-round candidates from the 64 entries received by the submission deadline of October 31, 2008. Submitters of the first-round candidates were invited to present their algorithms at the First SHA-3 Candidate Conference in Leuven, Belgium, in February 2009. Based on the reviews from the international cryptographic community, CSD selected 14 second-round candidates on July 24, 2009, and allowed submitters of the second-round candidates to make minor adjustments to their algorithms by September 15, 2009. The second round of the competition started in October 2009.

CSD held the Second SHA-3 Candidate Conference at the University of California, Santa Barbara, in August 2010 to discuss the security and performance analyses of the second-round candidates. CSD received significant feedback from the cryptographic community both before and after the conference. Some of the research was funded by the American Recovery and Reinvestment Act. Based on the public feedback and internal review, CSD selected five SHA-3 finalists on December 9, 2010, ending the second round of the competition. A status report of the second round was published on February 16, 2011.

Submitters of the SHA-3 finalists were allowed to make minor adjustments to their algorithms by January 16, 2011, and the third (and final) round of the competition began on January 31, 2011. A one-year public review period was allocated for the finalists. CSD plans to host the Third SHA-3 Candidate Conference on March 22-23, 2012, in Washington, D.C., where the results of community review and analysis of the finalists will be presented. Based on this public feedback and internal review, CSD intends to select the SHA-3 winner in summer 2012 and complete the competition. The then-current Secure Hash Standard will be revised to incorporate the winning SHA-3 algorithm.

http://www.nist.gov/hash-competition
Contact:
    Ms. Shu-jen Chang
    (301) 975-2940
    shu-jen.chang@nist.gov

Block Cipher Modes of Operation

The engine for many of the techniques in NIST's cryptographic toolkit is a block cipher algorithm, such as the Advanced Encryption Standard (AES) algorithm or the Triple Data Encryption Algorithm (TDEA). A block cipher transforms data of a fixed length, called the block size, into seemingly random data of the same length. There are different methods that feature block ciphers to achieve an information service such as confidentiality or authentication. Such a method is called a block cipher mode of operation, or, simply, a mode.

In 2010-2011, a previously approved mode was augmented, and three publications for new modes were in development.

In October 2010, an addendum to SP 800-38A, *Recommendation for Block Cipher Modes of Operation: Methods and Techniques*, was published. The addendum contained three variants of the Cipher Block Chaining (CBC) mode that employ the "ciphertext stealing" padding method. Plain CBC mode requires input messages whose length is a multiple of the block size; the variants extend this domain to messages of any length that is not strictly smaller than the block size. With conventional padding methods, the length of the ciphertext expands by the number of padding bits; the ciphertext stealing variants are designed to avoid such expansion.

One set of modes in development was in the area of "key wrapping," i.e., the protection of the confidentiality and integrity of cryptographic keys. In August 2011, NIST initiated a period of public comment on Draft SP 800-38F, *Recommendation for Block Cipher Modes of Operation: Methods for Key Wrapping*. In addition to describing existing approved methods, this draft publication specified three deterministic authenticated encryption modes: the AES Key Wrap (KW) mode, the AES Key Wrap With Padding (KWP) mode, and one TDEA mode, called TKW. Final publication is expected in the coming year.

A second set of modes in development is in the area of "format preserving encryption" (FPE). A format might be a credit card number or a social security number. FPE is expected to be very useful for retrofitting encryption to applications in a way that targets the sensitive data while minimizing the disruption to the data pathways in the application. Without FPF, the costs of providing confidentiality to sensitive data within an installed base can be prohibitive.

In the past couple of years, specifications for three FPE modes were submitted to NIST. After receiving acceptable Letters of Assurance from the submitters with respect to the licensing of potentially relevant patents, NIST initiated a period of public comment in June 2011 on a proposal to approve two schemes of the FFX (Format-preserving, Feistel-based) mode. Public comments supported the proposal, including many comments from the payments industry. A draft Special Publication for FPE methods is expected to be ready for public comment early next year.

A third mode in development is the EAX' mode for authenticated encryption with associated data. EAX' is specified in ANSI C12.22-2008, *American National*

Standard Protocol Specification for Interfacing to Data Communication Networks. That standard was developed by the American National Standards Institute (ANSI) C12 SC17 Committee, for which the National Electrical Manufacturers Association (NEMA) is the secretariat.

EAX' was developed for Smart Grid. In particular, EAX' was intended to satisfy the requirements of supervisory control and data acquisition (SCADA) messaging associated with Automated Meter Reading that operate in the context of an Advanced Metering Infrastructure. These requirements may be applicable to other small embedded devices communicating in SCADA environments. More information on the Smart Grid Cyber Security project is available on page 13.

In June 2011, NIST initiated a period of public comment on a proposal to approve EAX' and almost every comment supported the proposal. A draft SP for EAX' is expected to be ready for public comment next year.

Contact:
Dr. Morris Dworkin
(301) 975-2354
morris.dworkin@nist.gov

Key Management

NIST continues to address cryptographic key management for the federal government, and to coordinate this guidance with other national and international organizations, industry and academia. This guidance has been published as Special Publications (SPs), which are available at http://csrc.nist.gov/publications/PubsSPs.html.

To assist agencies and to recognize the speed at which the use of cryptography is changing, NIST published SP 800-131A, *Recommendation for the Transitioning of Cryptographic Algorithms and Key Sizes*. This publication provides additional details about the transition plan that was originally discussed in the key management guidance provided in SP 800-57, *Recommendation for Key Management, Part 1*, discussing the circumstances under which a particular algorithm and key length can be used or should be discontinued. The CSD has presented this plan at various forums and conferences. To help the vendors and testers of the cryptographic modules containing these algorithms deal with the upcoming transitions, CSD prepared a validation transition document that covers, from the vendor's and the testing laboratory's point of view, the affected algorithms.

SP 800-56A specifies approved methods for key establishment, using Diffie-Hellman and Menezes-Qu-Vanstone (MQV) schemes. This document, which was first published in 2006, is being revised to provide further clarification and an additional method for key derivation. This new method is specified in SP 800-56C, which was provided for public comment in FY2011, and will be completed in early FY2012. Another related publication, SP 800-135, *Recommendation for Existing Application-Specific Key Derivation Functions*, was completed in December 2010; this document approves existing application-specific key derivation functions used in protocols.

SP 800-57, Part 1, which provides general key management guidance, was first published in 2005, and later revised in 2007. This document is being updated to include information on and references to recent work performed by CSD; the document was posted for public comment in May 2011. SP 800-57, Part 3, which was published in 2009 and provides application-specific key management guidance, is being revised to reflect recent work on the applications and protocols discussed in the document and to include additional sections on the SSH protocol and the use of Trusted Platform Modules (TPMs).

SP 800-130, *A Framework for Designing Cryptographic Key Management Systems*, is being developed to provide guidance on the framework of a Cryptographic Key Management System (CKMS). The first draft of this document was posted for public comment in 2010 and was discussed in a subsequent workshop at NIST in late FY2010. During FY2011, the document was revised to address those comments, and work on a basic profile of the framework for the federal government was begun. The profile is intended to provide refinements of the framework requirements that are appropriate for use in a CKMS used by the federal government. See CSD's FY2010 report (http://csrc.nist.gov/publications/nistir/ir7751/nistir-7751_2010-csd-annual-report.pdf) and http://csrc.nist.gov/groups/ST/key_mgmt/ for background information on this project.

SP 800-132, *Recommendation for Password-Based Key Derivation Part 1: Storage Applications*, specifies approved techniques for the derivation of keys from passwords in order to protect electronic data in storage environments (e.g., laptop computers). The document was completed in December 2010.

SP 800-133, *Recommendation for Cryptographic Key Generation*, which discusses the generation of the keys to be managed and used by NIST's approved cryptographic algorithms, was issued for public comment in August 2011. It addresses the generation of a key using the output of a random bit generator, the derivation of a key from another key, the derivation of a key from a password, and keys generated during the use of a key-agreement scheme.

Many of these methods are specified in detail in other documents; SP 800-133 is intended for use as an overall "umbrella" document for key generation.

Below are the proposed plans for FY2012 for this project:

- SP 800-56A revision: Continue to revise and provide for public comment;

- SP 800-56B: Begin modifications similar to those for SP 800-56A;

- SP 800-56C: Post as a finished document;

- SP 800-57, Part 1 revision: Post as a finished document;

- SP 800-57, Part 3: Provide for public comment and post as a finished document;

- SP 800-130 and the federal profile: Provide for public comment and host a workshop to discuss the documents;

- SP 800-131A: Some of the remaining validation details associated with the transitions will be published in FY2012; and,

- SP 800-133: Address public comments and post as a completed document.

SPs: http://csrc.nist.gov/publications/PubsSPs.html
Key mgmt.: http://csrc.nist.gov/groups/ST/key_mgmt/
Contacts:

Ms. Elaine Barker	Mr. Quynh Dang
(301) 975-2911	(301) 975-3610
ebarker@nist.gov	qdang@nist.gov
Dr. Lily Chen	Dr. Meltem Sönmez Turan
(301) 975-6974	(301) 975-4391
llchen@nist.gov	meltem.turan@nist.gov
Dr. Allen Roginsky	
(301) 975-3603	
roginsky@nist.gov	

Security Guidelines Using Approved Hash Algorithms

Draft Federal Information Processing Standard (FIPS) 180-4, Secure Hash Standard (SHS)

FIPS 180-3, *Secure Hash Standard (SHS)*, specifies secure hash algorithms (SHAs) called SHA-1, SHA-224, SHA-256, SHA-384 and SHA-512. These algorithms produce 160, 224, 256, 384, and 512-bit outputs, respectively, which are called message digests. Draft FIPS 180-4 provides a general procedure for creating an initialization hash value, adds two additional secure hash algorithms, SHA-512/224 and SHA-512/256, to the standard, and removes a restriction that padding must be done before hash computation begins, which was required in FIPS 180-3. SHA-512/224 and SHA-512/256 may be more efficient alternatives to SHA-224 and SHA-256 on platforms that are optimized for 64-bit operations. Removing the restriction on padding operation in the secure hash algorithms will potentially allow more flexibility and efficiency in implementing the secure hash algorithms in many computer network applications.

On February 11, 2011, NIST published a notice in the Federal Register (76 FR 7817) announcing the availability of draft FIPS 180-4 and soliciting comments on the draft standard. Comments were received and are being addressed. FIPS 180-4 is expected to be approved in the near future.

NIST will submit the FIPS to the Secretary of Commerce for approval in the first half of FY2012.

NIST Draft (revised) SP 800-107, Recommendation for Applications Using Approved Hash Algorithms

SP 800-107 provides security guidelines for achieving the desired security strengths for cryptographic applications that employ the approved cryptographic hash functions specified in FIPS 180. The current version of this document was published in February 2009.

Draft FIPS 180-4 added two new hash algorithms: SHA-512/224 and SHA-512/256. SP 800-107 was revised to address the security properties of these new hash algorithms. Additional security information about hash message authentication code (HMAC) was added to provide stronger security guidance, and the hash-based key derivation function section was rewritten to provide updated information about approved hash-based key derivation functions specified in many other NIST SPs. The revised draft SP 800-107 was published in September 2011.

NIST will resolve comments and publish an updated version of the document in FY2012.

Contacts:

Ms. Elaine Barker	Mr. Quynh Dang
(301) 975-2911	(301) 975-3610
ebarker@nist.gov	qdang@nist.gov

Random Number Generator (RNG)

Random numbers are needed to provide the required security for most cryptographic algorithms. For example, random numbers are used to generate the keys needed for encryption and digital signature applications.

In the late 1990s, a project to develop more rigorous requirements and specifications for random number generation was begun in coordination with the American National Standards Institute's (ANSI) Accredited Standards Committee (ASC) X9. The resulting standard (X9.82) is being developed in four parts: Part 1 provides general information; Part 2 will provide requirements for entropy sources; Part 3 provides specifications for deterministic random bit generator (DRBG) mechanisms; and Part 4 will provide guidance on designing random bit generators (RBGs) from entropy sources and DRBG mechanisms. Parts 1 and 3 have been completed; Parts 2 and 4 are nearing completion.

In March 2007, NIST published SP 800-90, *Recommendation for Random Number Generation Using Deterministic Random Bit Generators*, which contained the DRBG mechanisms in Part 3 of X9.82, plus one additional DRBG mechanism.

During the development of Part 4 of X9.82, several changes for SP 800-90 were identified. In May 2011, a revision of SP 800-90 was provided for public comment as SP 800-90A that included these changes. Both SP 800-90 and SP 800-90A are available at http://csrc.nist.gov/publications/PubsSPs.html. The document number for SP 800-90 was modified so that two additional documents (i.e., SP 800-90B and SP 800-90C) could be included in a series on random number generation.

SP 800-90B will address entropy sources, pointing to Part 2 of X9.82 for design requirements, but also including descriptions of the validation tests that will be used by NIST's Cryptographic Algorithm Validation Program to validate entropy sources.

SP 800-90C will provide basic guidance on the construction of RBGs from entropy sources and DRBG mechanisms, pointing to Part 4 of X9.82 for additional constructions and examples.

NIST's standards activities in 2012 will include continued participation in ANSI X9 and progression of the different parts of SP 800-90. In ANSI, the goal will be completion of X9.82, Parts 2 and 4 in preparation for ANSI balloting. NIST expects to publish SP 800-90A after incorporating the public comments. NIST also plans to publish drafts of SP 800-90B and SP 800-90C for public comment in 2012.

SP 800-90 and SP 800-90A:
http://csrc.nist.gov/publications/PubsSPs.html
Contacts:

Ms. Elaine Barker	John Kelsey
(301) 975-2911	(301) 975-5101
ebarker@nist.gov	john.kelsey@nist.gov

Quantum Computing

Quantum computing, which uses quantum mechanical phenomena to perform operations on data, has the potential to become a major disruptive technology affecting cryptography and cryptanalysis given the potential increase in computing speed and power over conventional transistor-based computing. While a scalable quantum computing architecture has not been built, the physics and mathematics governing what can be done by a quantum computer are fairly well understood, and several algorithms have already been written for a quantum computing platform. Two of these algorithms are specifically applicable to cryptanalysis. Grover's quantum algorithm for database search potentially gives a quadratic speedup to brute-force cryptanalysis of block ciphers and hash functions. Grover's algorithm may, therefore, have a long-term effect on the necessary key lengths and digest sizes required for the secure operation of cryptographic protocols.

An even larger threat is presented by Shor's quantum algorithms for discrete logarithms and factorization. Given a quantum computer large enough to perform simple cryptographic operations, Shor's algorithm provides a practical computational mechanism for solving the two ostensibly hard problems that underlie all widely used public key cryptographic primitives. In particular, all the digital signature algorithms and public key-based key establishment schemes that are currently approved by NIST would be rendered insecure by the presence of even a fairly primitive quantum computer.

While practical quantum computers are not expected to be built in the next decade or so, it seems inevitable that they will eventually be built. NIST is responding to this eventuality by researching cryptographic algorithms for public key-based key agreement and digital signatures that are not susceptible to cryptanalysis by quantum algorithms. In the event that such algorithms cannot be found, NIST intends to draft standards for computer security architectures that do not rely on public key cryptographic primitives. In addition, NIST will examine new approaches, such as quantum key distribution.

On October 27-29, 2010, NIST, along with the University of Maryland's Joint Quantum Institute, held a workshop: "*From Quantum Information and Complexity to Post Quantum Information Security*." The NIST Computer Security Division (CSD) invited speakers on a number of apparently quantum-resistant technologies, including lattice-based, coding-based, and multivariate cryptography. In August 2011, the results of CSD-funded research on the coding-based McEliece cryptosystem were presented at the 31st International Cryptology Conference (Crypto 2011).

This research studied the asymptotic performance/security trade-off of McEliece and improved upon the best known attack using a technique called "ball collision decoding." Towards the end of FY2011, NIST also expanded its research program to examine the potential of multivariate cryptosystems and to study quantum algorithms. During this period, NIST researcher Daniel Smith-Tone published the paper, "On the Differential Security of Multivariate Public Key Cryptosystems," to be presented at PQCrypto2011, which takes place in Taipei from November 29, 2011 to December 2, 2011.

NIST will continue to study security technologies that may be resistant to attack by quantum computers, especially those that have generated some degree of commercial impact. If any of these technologies emerge as both commercially viable and widely trusted within the cryptographic community, NIST hopes to move towards standardization.

Contact:
 Mr. Ray Perlner
 (301) 975-3357
 ray.perlner@nist.gov

Authentication

To support the Office of Management and Budget (OMB) Memorandum M-04-04, E-Authentication Guidance for Federal Agencies, NIST developed SP 800-63, *Electronic Authentication Guideline*. The OMB policy memorandum defines four levels of authentication in terms of assurance about the validity of an asserted identity. SP 800-63 gives technical requirements and examples of authentication technologies that work by making individuals demonstrate possession and control of a secret for each of the four levels.

NIST is in the process of updating and revising SP 800-63 and has issued three drafts. Extensive comments have been received that reflect the extent to which SP 800-63 has been adopted by both the U.S. government and nonfederal users, including foreign governments and international standards bodies. The comments indicate a number of applications that were not anticipated in the original version or in the draft. The most difficult issues involve proposed new methods for reaching the highest authentication level, with current technologies. Comments on drafts, along with discussions in workshops and meetings, raised concerns with the password entropy and identity-proofing requirements as well as the relationship between SP 800-63 and other NIST identity-related activities such as FIPS 201-1, *Personal Identity Verification*

(PIV) of Federal Employees and Contractors, in support of Homeland Security Presidential Directive 12 (HSPD-12) and the National Strategy for Trusted Identities in Cyberspace (NSTIC). These concerns are being addressed in the final publication, expected no later than the first quarter of FY2012.

Through NIST's identity-related projects and hosting the IDTrust Symposium, several areas have emerged as key gaps in progressing secure authentication online: revocation in complex federated environments and biometric authentication in unattended scenarios. In federated environments, credential revocation has traditionally been managed by the credential issuer. In an effort to improve credential revocation mechanisms across federations and effectively mitigate credential misuse, NIST researchers are exploring the broader scope of credential revocation, where all parties contribute to and participate in credential revocation. In this model, service providers give feedback on a credential reliability score based on detected credential misuse. The credential holder and Identity Provider, on the other hand, receive feedback notification and are able to immediately suspend or revoke the credential should the score reach an unacceptable level. Lastly, other federated services can consult score and status to determine the suitability of a presented credential with an associated reliability score.

To address the use of biometrics in authentication for transactions online, NIST is considering high-level requirements for the use of biometrics in a multi-factor authentication framework, such as liveness detection (anti-spoofing methods), biometric template protection (for revoking and renewing biometric credentials), and web services standards for securely and uniformly handling biometric data online. Second, NIST is leading the development of an international web services standard, as well as the first standard on liveness detection. This latter will set the foundation for a common understanding of techniques, performance evaluation, and common data formats.

Contacts:
 Dr. Elaine Newton   Mr. Ray Perlner
 (301) 975-2532   (301) 975-3357
 elaine.newton@nist.gov   ray.perlner@nist.gov

 Ms. Hildegard Ferraiolo
 (301) 975-6972
 hildegard.ferraiolo@nist.gov

Security Aspects of Electronic Voting

In 2002, Congress passed the Help America Vote Act (HAVA) to encourage the upgrade of voting equipment across the United States. HAVA established the Election Assistance Commission (EAC) and the Technical Guidelines Development Committee (TGDC), chaired by the Director of NIST. HAVA calls on NIST to provide technical support to the EAC and TGDC in efforts related to human factors, security, and laboratory accreditation. As part of NIST's efforts, CSD supports the activities of the EAC and the TGDC related to voting equipment security.

In the past year, we supported the efforts of the EAC and Federal Voting Assistance Program (FVAP) of DoD to improve the voting process for citizens under the Uniformed and Overseas Citizens Voting Act (UOCAVA) by leveraging electronic technologies. This work included the development of the following documents: NISTIR 7682, *IT Security Best Practices for UOCAVA Supporting Voting Systems*; NISTIR 7711, *Security Best Practices for the Electronic Distribution of Election Materials*; and NISTIR 7770, *Security Considerations for Remote Electronic UOCAVA Voting*. We worked with the TDCG's UOCAVA Working Group to develop aspirational high-level goals for UOCAVA voting systems, and identified possible pilot voting systems for the 2012 and 2014 elections. In addition, we supported the EAC in updating the Voluntary Voting System Guidelines (VVSG), VVSG 1.1, by assisting the EAC with resolutions to comments and developing a new draft of the guidelines for public comment. Our work on voting technologies has also spun off interesting research topics, including the Rabin Beacon project that is discussed separately in this annual report.

In FY2012, we expect to finalize the VVSG 1.1 and its associated security test suites. We will continue to support the efforts for the EAC and FVAP to improve the voting process for UOCAVA voters. We will continue to conduct research on threats to voting systems, innovative voting system architectures, and the Rabin Beacon project. In addition, we will support the NIST National Voluntary Laboratory Accreditation Program (NVLAP) efforts to accredit voting system test laboratories by developing proficiency tests and testing artifacts. We plan to engage voting system manufacturers, voting system test laboratories, state election officials, and the academic community in exploring ways to increase voting system security and transparency.

http://vote.nist.gov/
Contacts:

Dr. Nelson Hastings	Mr. Andrew Regenscheid
(301) 975-5237	(301) 975-5155
nelson.hastings@nist.gov	andrew.regenscheid@nist.gov

Development of Federal Information Processing Standard (FIPS) 140-3, Security Requirements for Cryptographic Modules

The FIPS 140 standard is applicable to all federal agencies that use cryptography-based security systems to protect sensitive information in computer and telecommunication systems (including voice systems) as defined in Section 5131 of the Information Technology Management Reform Act of 1996, Public Law 104-106 and the Federal Information Security Management Act of 2002, Public Law 107-347. The standard must be used in designing and implementing cryptographic modules that federal departments and agencies operate or are operated for them under contract.

Draft FIPS 140-3, *Security Requirements for Cryptographic Modules*, provides four increasing qualitative levels of security that are intended to cover a wide range of potential applications and environments. The security requirements cover areas related to the secure design and implementation of a cryptographic module. These areas include cryptographic module specification; cryptographic module physical ports and logical interfaces; roles, authentication, and services; software security; operational environment; physical security; physical security – non-invasive attacks; sensitive security parameter management; self-tests; life-cycle assurance; and mitigation of other attacks. The standard provides users with a specification of security features that are required at each of four security levels, flexibility in choosing security requirements, a guide to ensuring that the cryptographic modules incorporate necessary security features, and the assurance that the modules are compliant with cryptography-based standards.

The FIPS 140-3 draft is a result of the reexamination and reaffirmation of the current standard, FIPS 140-2. The draft standard adds new security requirements imposed on cryptographic modules to reflect the latest advances in technology and security, and to mirror other new or updated standards published by NIST in the area of cryptography and key management. Additionally, software and firmware requirements are addressed in a new area dedicated to software and firmware security, while another new area specifying requirements to protect against non-invasive attacks is also provided.

The development of FIPS 140-3 started in 2005 and relies on the preliminary inputs provided by users, testing laboratories, and vendors during the September 2004 NIST-CSE Cryptographic Module Validation Symposium and the September 2005 NIST-CSE Physical Security Workshop. CSE is the Canadian government's Communications Security Establishment. In 2007, the first draft of the standard was released for public comment, and NIST received over 1,200 comments, which were thoroughly reviewed and discussed, and the working group's resolutions were implemented in the second draft of the standard. In December 2009, the second draft of the standard was released for public comment, and NIST received over 900 comments, which were analyzed, discussed and addressed by the NIST Technical Working Group (TWG) in the latest draft (the third) of the standard.

During FY2011, the Federal Register Notice announcing the changes made in the third draft of the FIPS 140-3 standard in response to the public comments received on the second draft was prepared and submitted for approval. The TWG finalized implementing the resolutions to the public comments received on the second draft and prepared the standard for a NIST and CSE Canada final technical internal review. All comments received from the internal reviewers were addressed, and the document was then prepared for the management's review. A Federal Register Notice that announces the changes made in the third draft is being prepared. The changes include: description of the assumed thread models for each security level; insertion of missing definitions for terms and acronyms; Trusted Channel requirements; removal of the Trusted Role; allowing identity-based authentication mechanism at Security level (SL) 2; insertion of the self-initiated cryptographic output capability and of the remote control capability; additional integrity techniques requirements for software components of a cryptographic; and restructuring of the annexes while enhancing the requirements for the allowed operator authentication mechanisms, the list of the non-invasive attacks methods for the security functions, and the requirements for the allowed modifiable operating environments.

The Federal Register Notice that announces the changes made in the third draft of the FIPS 140-3 standard will be finalized and submitted for approval. Following the public comments period, the TWG will address all comments received and prepare the document for publication.

http://csrc.nist.gov/groups/ST/FIPS140_3/
Contact:
  Dr. Michaela Iorga
  (301) 975-8431
  michaela.iorga@nist.gov

NIST Beacon – A Prototype Implementation of a Randomness Beacon

NIST is implementing a trusted public source of randomness, conformant to SP 800-90, *Recommendation for Random Number Generation Using Deterministic Random Bit Generators*. The source is designed to provide *unpredictability, autonomy, and consistency*. *Unpredictability* means that users cannot algorithmically predict bits before they are made available by the source. *Autonomy* means that the source is resistant to attempts by outside parties to alter the distribution of the random bits. *Consistency* means that a set of users can access the source in such a way that they are confident that they all receive the same random string.

The theoretical community has developed many creative cryptographic security protocols over the years for access, authentication, privacy, and authorization in networking and e-commerce applications. However, except for the simplest and most basic protocols, few have been widely deployed. A major reason concerns efficiency. Many of the more sophisticated security protocols, such as Zero Knowledge proof systems, are highly interactive and require too many communication rounds to be feasible in most situations. Other privacy-preserving protocols eliminate the need for many rounds of communication but assume the availability of a trusted source of randomness, an assumption that is not generally valid at present.

In response, NIST is developing a Secure Randomness Beacon that is broadcasting full-entropy bit-strings. We plan to post them in blocks of 512 bits every ΔT seconds, where ΔT is an adjustable parameter that can vary from one second to minutes. Each such value is sequence-numbered, time-stamped and signed, and includes the hash of the previous value to chain the sequence of values together and prevent even the source to retroactively change an output package without being detected. The beacon will keep all output packets and make them available online.

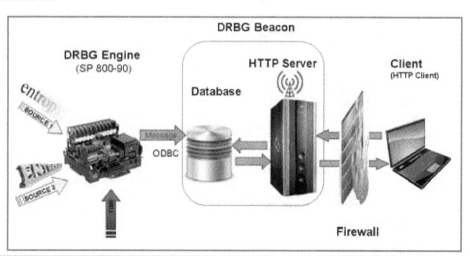

The beacon's engine uses multiple input sources of entropy, and the NIST team leveraged recent work done on tests to validate an entropy source.

During the next year, NIST will continue working on implementing and enhancing the NIST Secure Randomness Beacon and provide a publicly available proof-of-concept that users can trust. NIST's Physics Laboratory will assist us in enhancing the input sources on entropy to the beacon's engine by adding at least one quantum source.

Contact:
Dr. Michaela Iorga
(301) 975-8431
michaela.iorga@nist.gov

Cryptography for Emerging Technologies and Applications (CETA) Workshop

The *CETA Workshop* will provide an opportunity for industry, research and academia communities, and government sectors to identify cryptographic challenges encountered in their development of emerging technologies and applications, and to learn about NIST's current cryptographic research, activities, programs, and standards development. Technology areas to be addressed include sensor and building networks, mobile devices, smart objects/Internet of things, and cyber physical systems.

NIST considered the following trends when organizing the CETA Workshop: the increasing demand for small footprint cryptography for power-constrained devices; the emerging desire, from both providers and consumers, for trustworthy processes supporting secure communications and transactions that maximize integrity and non-repudiation properties on single end-user devices that access many kinds of services and applications, and the need for individual users that access the same services and applications from multiple platforms; the need for much more agile key management on cyberspace; and the need for usable and reliable public, enterprise-specific, pseudonymous, and anonymous modes of operation from the same end-user device.

In preparation for the workshop, NIST called for the submission of abstracts. The abstracts must highlight cryptographic challenges identified during the research and development of emerging technologies and applications.

Examples of emerging or evolving technology areas include:
- Sensor and building networks;
- Mobile devices;
- Smart Objects/Internet of Things; and
- Cyber physical systems.

Examples of cryptographic requirements for emerging sectors might include: performance or resource issues; cryptographic services (such as anonymous or group signatures); or key management challenges.

The workshop on *Cryptography for Emerging Technologies and Applications (CETA)* will be hosted on November 7-8, 2011 in Gaithersburg, Maryland. Prior to the workshop, all submitted abstracts will be posted on NIST's website, and the authors of selected abstracts will be invited to present their work during the workshop.

http://www.nist.gov/itl/csd/ct/ceta-workshop.cfm
Contact:
Dr. Michaela Iorga
(301) 975-8431
michaela.iorga@nist.gov

Pairing-Based Cryptography

Recently, what are known as pairings on elliptic curves have been a very active area of research in cryptography. A pairing is a function which maps a pair of points on an elliptic curve into a finite field. Their unique properties have enabled many new cryptographic protocols that had not previously been feasible.

In particular, identity-based encryption (IBE) is a pairing-based scheme which has received much attention. IBE is the concept of using some form of personal identification to generate a public key. This could be an email address, for instance. An IBE scheme allows a sender to encrypt a message without needing a receiver's public key to have been certified and distributed for subsequent use. Such a scenario is quite useful if the pre-distribution of public keys is impractical. Besides IBE, there are a number of other applications of pairing-based cryptography. These include many other identity-based cryptosystems (including signature schemes), key establishment schemes, functional and attribute-based encryption, and privacy-enhancing techniques, such as the use of anonymous credentials.

In 2008, NIST held a workshop on pairing-based cryptography. While the workshop showed that there was interest in pairing-based schemes, a common understanding was that further study was needed before NIST approved any such schemes. Throughout 2011, members of the Cryptographic Technology Group conducted an extensive study on pairing-based cryptographic schemes. This included topics such as: the construction of pairing-friendly elliptic curves; a survey of pairing-based cryptographic schemes; the implementation efficiency with respect to the required security; standard activities involving pairing-based schemes; use cases; and practical implications. This work is being summarized in a technical report, which will be presented in early 2012.

Contacts:

Dr. Dustin Moody
(301) 975-8136
dustin.moody@nist.gov

Dr. Lily Chen
(301) 975-6974
lily.chen@nist.gov

Personal Identity Verification (PIV) Test Cards

Federal Information Processing Standard (FIPS) 201, *Personal Identity Verification (PIV) of Federal Employees and Contractors*, was published in February 2005 to satisfy policy directives specified in Homeland Security Presidential Directive 12 (HSPD-12). The majority of federal workers now have Personal Identity Verification (PIV) cards; however, the PIV card has not yet been embraced as a mechanism for logical access to IT resources. Unavailability of PIV test cards has been identified as an impediment to deployment.

In order to facilitate the development of applications and middleware that support the PIV card, CSD is developing a reference set of smart cards. This set of test cards will include not only examples that are similar to cards that are currently issued today, but also examples of cards with features that are expected to appear in cards that will be issued in the future. For example, while the certificates and data objects on most, if not all, cards issued today are signed using RSA Public-Key Cryptography Standard (PKCS) #1 v1.5, the set of test cards will include examples of certificates and data objects that are signed using each of the algorithms and key sizes approved for use with PIV cards, including the RSA Probabilistic Signature Scheme (RSASSA-PSS) and the Elliptic Curve Digital Signature Algorithm (ECDSA). Similarly, the infrastructure supporting the test cards will provide examples of Certificate Revocation Lists (CRLs) and Online Certificate Status Protocol (OCSP) responses that are signed using each of these signature algorithms. The set of test cards also will include certificates with elliptic curve cryptography (ECC) subject public keys in addition to RSA subject public keys, as is permitted by Table 3-1 of SP 800-78-3, *Interfaces for Personal Identity Verification*. The set of test cards, collectively, will also include all of the mandatory and optional data objects listed in Section 3 of SP 800-73-3 Part 1, except for Cardholder Iris Images. Several of the cards will include a Key History object along with retired key management keys. The certificates that appear on the test cards, both the card holders' certificates and the content signers' certificates, will be issued from a simple two-level hierarchy.

During FY2011, CSD developed an initial specification for the set of test PIV cards. The initial specification calls for the set to include sixteen cards, nine valid cards and seven cards that contain invalid data. The valid cards differ in terms of the cryptographic algorithms used to sign the data objects, the types and sizes of the card holder's key pairs, and in the presence or absence of optional data objects. The invalid cards include cards that are expired, cards that have certificates that have been revoked, and cards with data objects that have invalid signatures.

CSD also extended the capabilities of the PIV Data Generator to be able to generate all of the data objects associated with the test cards and extended the capabilities of the PIV Data Loader to be able to load all of the certificates, key pairs, and other data objects associated with the test cards onto blank card stock. The keys and data for the test cards were generated along with the infrastructure needed to support these cards, and one set of test cards was generated for use in internal testing.

Early in FY2012, a few sets of test cards will be generated based on the initial specification, and these sets of test cards will be distributed to organizations that have previously volunteered to serve as beta testers. Feedback from the beta testers will be used to determine whether any changes need to be made to the final specification for the sets of test cards. Sets of test cards based on the final specification will then be created and made available for purchase.

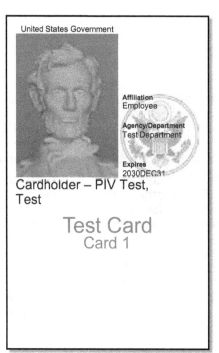

United States Government

Affiliation
Employee

Agency/Department
Test Department

Expires
2030DEC31

Cardholder – PIV Test, Test

Test Card
Card 1

Contacts:

Dr. David Cooper
(301) 975-3194
david.cooper@nist.gov

Mr. William Polk
(301) 975-3348
william.polk@nist.gov

BIOS Security

Modern computers rely on fundamental system firmware, commonly known as the Basic Input/Output System (BIOS), to facilitate the hardware initialization process and transition control to the operating system. The BIOS is a security-critical component because of its unique and privileged position within modern computers. A malicious BIOS modification could be part of a sophisticated, targeted attack on an organization—either a permanent denial of service (if the BIOS is corrupted) or a persistent malware presence (if the BIOS is implanted with malware). As security in operating systems and applications has improved, a race to "bare metal" has begun between those wishing to attack systems and those responsible for protecting them. Attacks on the BIOS are an evolving threat area that could become a future battlefront.

To combat this threat, in FY2011, NIST began a new project to secure the BIOS. As the computer industry is currently transitioning to BIOS based on the Unified Extensible Firmware Interface (UEFI), a recent industry specification for system firmware, NIST had the opportunity to influence the next generation of systems. For the past year, NIST has been working with key members of the computer industry on mechanisms to improve the security of the BIOS.

In April 2011, NIST issued SP 800-147, *BIOS Protection Guidelines*, which provides guidance on protecting the BIOS in laptop and desktop computers. This document provides platform vendors with recommendations and guidelines for a secure BIOS update process. Additionally, it provides system administrators and information system security professionals with recommendations for managing the BIOS in an operational environment.

SP 800-147 has already had a major impact due to an extraordinary response from hardware and software vendors in the computer industry. Within six months of publication of the *BIOS Protection Guidelines*, several major computer vendors were already offering products intended to meet the guidelines in that document.

In FY2012, NIST will continue its efforts to secure the system BIOS and other critical firmware. We plan to develop guidelines for protecting the BIOS in servers and boot firmware in computer add-on cards. We also plan to develop security requirements for systems designed to detect unauthorized changes to the BIOS and its configuration settings. These efforts to improve the security of the BIOS are intended to lay the foundation for secure systems. Future efforts will explore methods to extend trust in the security of the BIOS to provide greater assurance of the security of the operating system and applications.

Contact:
  Mr. Andrew Regenscheid
  (301) 975-5155
  andrew.regenscheid@nist.gov

Privacy Enhancing Cryptography Project

Modern cryptography provides powerful tools for protecting private information, but current standards are often blunt instruments for privacy protection. There are many ways we can develop and standardize new methods to use cryptography that enhance privacy. For example, public-key certificates used for authentication often reveal more personally identifiable information about the certificate holder than is required for many applications. What is often at issue in accessing data or resources is not the identity of the customer, but whether the customer is a member of the eligible group. Methods that allow a user to selectively reveal and prove only a specific property (such as age over 21, place of residence, or citizenship, etc.), are approaching commercial practicality.

Other techniques, such as those that will eventually allow us to search encrypted databases, are still in the research stage. But they are sufficiently advanced that it behooves us to take stock of the state of the art at this point. Still other techniques, such as those that allow us to hold sealed-bid auctions without ever opening the bids, are known to be practical, yet have received little attention by those that might benefit from them. Such applications fall within the scope of what are known as secure multiparty computations.

In FY2011, NIST held meetings with hardware and software manufacturers, including Microsoft's U-Prove team and Intel's Enhanced Privacy ID (EPID) team, to discuss privacy-enhancing technologies. Future meetings with additional organizations are being scheduled. Additionally, NIST published *Secure Sealed-Bid Online Auctions Using Discreet Cryptographic Proofs*, which discussed privacy-preserving auctions and several other papers on technical components of secure multiparty computation.

In December 2011, NIST will hold a workshop on Privacy-Enhancing Cryptographic Techniques to explore processes, procedures, and potential applications that could benefit from the ability to operate on encrypted data without decrypting it.

Contact:
  Dr. Rene Peralta
  (301) 975-8702
  peralta@nist.gov

Systems and Emerging Technologies Security Research Group

Strategic Goal

Devise advanced security methods, tools, and guidelines through conducting near-term and midterm security research.

Overview

In our security research, we focus on identifying emerging and high-priority technologies, and on developing security solutions that will have a high impact on the U.S. critical information infrastructure. We conduct research and development on behalf of government and industry from the earliest stages of technology development through proof-of-concept, reference and prototype implementations, and demonstrations. We work to transfer new technologies to industry, to produce new standards and guidance for federal agencies and industry, and to develop tests, test methodologies, and assurance methods.

Some of the many topics we investigate include mobile device security, security automation, cloud computing, identity management, access control and authorization management, Internet protocol (IP) security, software assurance, and vulnerability analysis. Our research helps to meet federal information security requirements that may not be fully addressed by existing technology. We collaborate extensively with government, academia, and private sector entities. In the past year, collaborations have included the National Security Agency (NSA), the Department of Defense (DoD), the Defense Advanced Research Projects Agency (DARPA), the Department of Homeland Security (DHS), the National Aeronautics and Space Administration (NASA), the U.S. Air Force, the University of Maryland, George Mason University, Purdue University, North Carolina State University, Johns Hopkins University Applied Physics Laboratory, Carnegie Mellon University, Microsoft Corporation, Intel, Symantec, Lockheed Martin, and MITRE.

Example successes from this work include tools for access control policy testing; new concepts in access control and policy enforcement; protocols, tools, and standards for security automation; IPv6 transition guidance; interoperability test suites for biometrics; methods for analyzing vulnerabilities in networks; operating system hardening plus test methods for mobile device (smart phone) security; and software assurance through

combinatorial testing. For the federal government's cloud computing initiatives, we produced use cases, publications, and definitions and guidance for cloud users and providers. To improve access to new technologies, we also chaired, edited, and participated in the development of a wide variety of national and international security standards.

Identity Management

Personal Identity Verification (PIV) and FIPS 201 Revision Efforts

In response to Homeland Security Presidential Directive 12 (HSPD-12), *Policy for a Common Identification Standard for Federal Employees and Contractors*, Federal Information Processing Standard (FIPS) 201, *Personal Identity Verification (PIV) of Federal Employees and Contractors*, was developed and was approved by the Secretary of Commerce in February 2005. HSPD-12 calls for the creation of a new identity credential for federal employees and contractors. FIPS 201 is the technical specification of both the new identity credential and the PIV system that produces, manages, and uses the credential. According to the Office of Management and Budget (OMB), as of June 2011, approximately 5 million federal employee and contractors (87 percent of the federal workforce) have been issued their PIV cards. This work is done in collaboration with the Cryptographic Technologies Group.

CSD activities in FY2011 directly supported the revision and maintenance of the FIPS 201 standard. CSD performed the following activities during FY2011 to revise the standard:

- Drafted and published a revision of FIPS 201 on March 8, 2011. Changes in the revision (i.e., FIPS 201-2) include clarifications to existing text, removal of conflicting requirements, additional text in cases where there were ambiguities, adaptation to changes in the marketplace since the publication of FIPS 201-1, and specific requests received from agencies and implementers. NIST coordinated with OMB and U.S. government (USG) stakeholders before incorporating changes in the draft FIPS 201-2. NIST also addressed business requirements for FIPS 201-2 gathered from the meeting on government requirements held in July 2010.

- Organized and facilitated a workshop to discuss the contents of revised FIPS 201. NIST held a two-day workshop on April 18-19, 2011, to discuss the contents of FIPS 201-2. The workshop was another mechanism to reach out to the PIV community, to interact with implementers and vendors, to clarify and explain new concepts in FIPS 201-2, and to encourage the PIV community to provide formal comments to NIST.

- Processed and analyzed comments received on FIPS 201-2. NIST started to review and process more than 1,000 comments received from over 40 organizations.

- Participated in stakeholder meetings and provided technical contributions to the Federal Identity Credential Access Management (FICAM) Architecture Working Group (AWG).

- Provided technical security controls to facilitate PIN caching for PIV systems in very specific environments.

In FY2012, we will focus on completing the revision of FIPS 201-2. We will also continue to provide technical and strategic inputs to the PIV-related initiatives.

http://csrc.nist.gov/groups/SNS/piv
Contacts:
Ms. Hildegard Ferraiolo   Mr. William I. MacGregor
(301) 975-6972
hildegard.ferraiolo@nist.gov

NIST Personal Identity Verification Program (PIV)

The objective of the NIST Personal Identity Verification Program (NPIVP) is to validate PIV components for conformance to specifications in FIPS 201 and its companion documents. The two PIV components that come under the scope of NPIVP are PIV Smart Card Application and PIV Middleware. All of the tests under NPIVP are handled by third-party laboratories that are accredited as Cryptographic and Security Testing (CST) Laboratories by the NIST National Voluntary Laboratory Accreditation Program (NVLAP) and are called accredited NPIVP test facilities. As of September 2011, there are ten such facilities.

In prior years, CSD published SP 800-85A, *PIV Card Application and Middleware Interface Test Guidelines*, to facilitate development of PIV Smart Card Application and PIV Middleware that conform to interface specifications in SP 800-73, *Interfaces for Personal Identity Verification*. We also developed an integrated toolkit called "PIV Interface

Test Runner" for conducting tests on both PIV Card Application and PIV Middleware products, and provided the toolkit to accredited NPIVP test facilities.

In 2010, the third edition of SP 800-73 (numbered as SP 800-73-3), was published. The same year, we updated and published SP 800-85A-1, *PIV Card Application and Middleware Interface Test Guidelines*, to provide test guidelines that align with SP 800-73-3.

In FY2011 and with the release of SP 800-73-3 in the prior year, NPIVP identified the necessary updates for the PIV Interface Test Runner to align with SP 800-73-3 and the revised PIV card interface test guidelines in SP 800-85A-2. The PIV Interface Test Runner was updated to perform additional tests needed for SP 800-73-3 compliance and was distributed to the ten accredited NPIVP test facilities in the first quarter of FY2011. With the introduction of the new Test Runner, the NPIVP test facilities now base their evaluations of PIV Card application and PIV Middleware products on the updated PIV Interface Test Runner.

In addition to the interface specification in SP 800-73-3, another NIST publication, SP 800-78, *Cryptographic Algorithms and Key Sizes for Personal Identity Verification*, specifies the PIV Card's cryptographic capability. This publication establishes approved cryptographic mechanisms for the PIV card and infrastructure. It also proposes sunset dates for cryptographic algorithms that are deemed less secure after a specific date. By the beginning of January 2011, for example, the 2-Key Triple DES algorithms (2TDEA) for the PIV card's optional Card Authentication Key (CAK) was discontinued to ensure adequate cryptographic strength for the PIV card. Instead of 2TDEA, higher-strength cryptographic algorithms are specified in SP 800-78-2, such as 3-Key Triple DES algorithms (3TDEA), AES 128, and others. In anticipation of the discontinuation of the 2TDEA for the affected PIV cards, NPIVP coordinated the upgrade to higher strength CAK and CMK, and provided revalidation guidelines for affected client products. Fortunately, no PIV Card Application products were affected by the discontinuation of 2 Key Triple DES, since validated PIV cards already had the capability to provide higher cryptographic strength for the CAK and CMK.

In FY2011, eight PIV card application products were validated for conformance to SP 800-73-2, three PIV card application products were validated for conformance to SP 800-73-3, and certificates were issued, bringing the total number of NPIVP-validated PIV Card application products to 28. The three PIV card application products validated for conformance to SP 800-73-3 were originally submitted for validation for conformance to SP 800-73-2 and later submitted for upgrade to SP 800-73-3 specifications. Three more PIV Middleware products were validated for conformance to SP 800-73-2 and were issued certificates, bringing the total number of NPIVP-validated PIV Middleware products that conform to SP 800-73-2 to 4 and the overall number of PIV Middleware products to 15.

http://csrc.nist.gov/groups/SNS/piv/npivp
Contacts:

Dr. Ramaswamy Chandramouli   Ms. Hildegard Ferraiolo
(301) 975-5013   (301) 975-6972
chandramouli@nist.gov   hildegard.ferraiolo@nist.gov

Conformity Assessment Program and Qualified Product List (QPL) for Identity and Credential Products for DHS/TSA

The Transportation Security Administration (TSA), an agency of the Department of Homeland Security (DHS), has a requirement to establish a process to qualify products and to maintain a Qualified Products List (QPL) for use within the Transportation Worker Identification Credential (TWIC) program as well as other DHS and TSA programs such as the U.S. Coast Guard that adopts, for their operations, identity and credential products conformant to the same standards and specifications.

The DHS has asked NIST to assist with the establishment of a conformity assessment framework in support of a Qualified Technologies List (QTL) for identity and privilege credential products, to be managed by DHS/TSA. Additionally, NIST is assisting with the establishment of a testing regime for the qualifying products for conformity to specified standards and TSA specifications.

This Conformity Assessment Program will provide credentials with heightened assurance at reduced cost. Approved credentials can be easily identified and procured by government (state, local, tribal), private entities (e.g., airports) and TSA grant receivers.

This work builds on ITL's Core Competency in IT standards development and deployment. As new specifications emerge, metrics and test methods need to be developed to support adoption of these technologies.

During FY2011, NIST's team, in collaboration with our contractors, finalized the QTL's Administrative Manual, the Approval Procedure, Derived Test Requirements, and Test Procedures documents, and developed a tool for testing smart card portable and fixed TWIC readers for conformance to the TWIC specification published in 2008.

NIST's team completed the project during FY2011.

Contact:
  Dr. Michaela Iorga
  (301) 975-8431
  michaela.iorga@nist.gov

Biometric Standards and Conformity Assessment Activities

The project responds to government, industry, and market requirements for open systems standards by: (a) accelerating development of formal biometric standards; (b) providing effective leadership and technical participation in the development of these standards; (c) developing Conformance Test Architectures and Test Suites designed to test implementations of biometric standards; (d) supporting harmonization of biometric, tokens and security standards; (e) promoting biometric standards adoption; and (f) promoting conformity assessment efforts.

CSD's staff continues to work in close partnership with government agencies, industry, and academic institutions to develop formal national and international biometric standards. CSD's staff actively participates in a number of biometric standards development projects, contributes to the development of biometric standards, and leads national[2] and international[3] biometric standards bodies. This work is planned to continue in FY2012.

We actively participate in the National Science and Technology Council Subcommittee on Biometrics and Identity Management and its Standards and Conformity Assessment Working Group as well as other U.S. government (USG) groups, such as DHS's Biometrics Working Group and DoD's Biometrics Identity Management Agency Biometric Standards Working Group.

We develop conformance test architectures (CTAs) and conformance test suites (CTSs) to support end-users in USG and other organizations, testing laboratories, and system integrators as well as product developers interested in conforming to biometric standards by using the same testing tools available to users[4]. Related activities and conformance test tool releases in previous years were discussed in preceding annual reports[5].

During FY2011, we released a number of conformance test suites (CTSs) designed to test implementations of biometric data interchange formats conforming to international standards, including two CTS versions of a

---

[2] InterNational Committee for Information Technology Standards (INCITS) Technical Committee 1 (M1) - *Biometrics* - INCITS M1 Public Website: http://standards.incits.org/a/public/group/m1

[3] Joint Technical Committee 1 (JTC 1) of the International Standards Organization (ISO) and the International Electrotechnical Commission (IEC) Subcommittee SC 37 - Biometrics - JTC 1/SC 37 Home Page: http://www.iso.org/iso/jtc1_sc37_home.html

[4] This work is sponsored, in part, by DHS/US-VISIT.

[5] CSD "2007 report" (pp. 44-47), CSD "2008 report" (pp. 30-34), CSD "2009 report" (pp. 31-33), and CSD "2010 report" (pp. 28-30). http://csrc.nist.gov/publications/PubsTC.html#Annual%20Reports

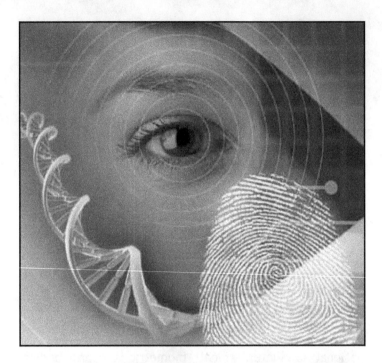

usability, and reliability, and provide rich test results information. We are also planning to address support for rich web services capabilities. The project will evolve from web services research, development, and testing to implementation.

We plan to continue supporting the Biometric Consortium which is co-chaired by a member of CSD's staff and a member of the National Security Agency's staff. The Biometric Consortium Conference, with participation of over 1,500 attendees, was held September 27-29, 2011.

ITL's Biometric resource Center:
http://www.nist.gov/biometrics

Conformance Test Tool Downloads:
http://www.nist.gov/itl/csd/biometrics/
biocta_download.cfm#CTAdownloads

Contact:
Mr. Fernando Podio
(301) 975-2947
fernando.podio@nist.gov

Research in Emerging Technologies

Automated Combinatorial Testing for Software

Software developers often encounter failures that result from an unexpected interaction between components. NIST research has shown that most failures are triggered by one or two parameters, and progressively fewer by three, four, or more parameters (see graph below), a relationship that we call the *interaction rule*. These results have important implications for testing. If all faults in a system can be triggered by a combination of *n* or fewer parameters, then testing all *n*-way combinations of parameters can provide very strong fault detection efficiency. These methods are being applied to software and hardware testing for reliability, safety, and security. Our focus is on empirical results and real-world problems.

tool designed to test implementations of the standardized iris image specification for the PIV Card and for off-card use of iris images as specified in draft SP 800-76-2[6]. This year we initiated support for the ANSI/NIST-ITL standards[7]. Two versions of a CTA/CTS designed to test implementations of the ANSI/NIST-ITL 1-2007 standard[8] were released. NIST Interagency Report (NISTIR) 7791[9] includes technical information on this test tool.

We are also supporting the development of the 2011 version of the ANSI/NIST-ITL standard (AN-2011) and an associated conformance testing methodology development. CSD's staff developed tables of requirements and test assertions for selected Record Types specified in the standard. Over 1,200 assertions were documented. NISTIR 7806[10] documents the assertions developed and the terms, operands, and operators used in defining these assertions.

Planned work for FY2012 and beyond includes development of CTSs to test implementations of international biometric data interchange formats under development in JTC 1/SC 37 (e.g., binary and XML data format encodings). Plans include development of advanced CTAs and CTSs to improve performance (e.g., multiple-thread implementations),

[6] DRAFT NIST Special Publication 800-76-2, *Biometric Data Specification for Personal Identity Verification*, NIST/ITL, P. Grother, W. Salamon, and J. Matey, April 17, 2011.

[7] ANSI/NIST-ITL standard "Data Format for the Interchange of Fingerprint, Facial & Other Biometric Information" home page: http://www.nist.gov/itl/iad/ig/ansi_standard.cfm

[8] NIST Special Publication 500-271, *ANSI/NIST-ITL 1-2007, American National Standard for Information Systems - Data Format for the Interchange of Fingerprint Facial, & Other Biometric Information – Part 1.*

[9] NISTIR 7791, *Conformance Test Architecture and Test Suite for ANSI/NIST-ITL 1-2007*, F. Podio, D. Yaga, and C. McGinnis, June 2011.

[10] NISTIR 7806, *ANSI/NIST-ITL 1-2011 Requirements and Conformance Test Assertions*, C. McGinnis, D. Yaga, and F. Podio, September 2011.

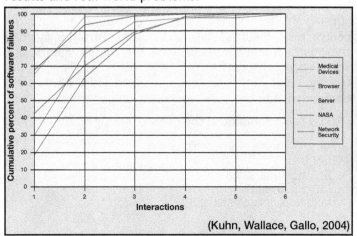

(Kuhn, Wallace, Gallo, 2004)

Technology development highlights for FY2011 included a case study demonstrating equivalent fault detection using less than five percent of the original number of tests for an interoperability standard; development of a new mathematical construct, *sequence covering arrays*, (jointly with U.S. Air Force [USAF]) for event sequence testing with demonstrations on USAF system testing; and development of a new tool for combinatorial coverage measurement.

Tech transfer activities included release of our comprehensive text, SP 800-142, *Practical Combinatorial Testing*, which has been downloaded by more than 11,000 users; publication of five technical papers; plus seminars and lectures at Carnegie Mellon University, NASA, Fraunhofer Institute, Institute for Defense Analysis, Department of Energy, The Technische Universität Berlin (T.U. Berlin), Indian Institute of Technology, and several conferences.

Plans for FY2012 include cooperative work with the NASA Independent Verification and Validation (IV&V) Facility investigating the effectiveness of combinatorial testing for IV&V of space systems; a significant expansion and new release of the text, *Practical Combinatorial Testing*; development of methods and tools for fault location; lectures at conferences and research labs; and release of a report with Cooperative Research and Development Agreement (CRADA) partner Lockheed Martin on use of these methods for aerospace software testing.

http://csrc.nist.gov/groups/SNS/acts/
Contacts:

Mr. Rick Kuhn	Dr. Raghu Kacker
(301) 975-3337	(301) 975-2109
kuhn@nist.gov	raghu.kacker@nist.gov

Cloud Computing and Virtualization

Cloud computing offers the possibility of increasing efficiency with a decrease in cost. However, as with any new technology, there are many questions about security. NIST is providing technical guidance and promoting standards supporting the effective and secure use of cloud computing within government and industry. Our first effort was to define cloud computing and its models. This guidance assists organizations in making informed decisions about procuring cloud services.

According to the NIST cloud computing definition: "Cloud computing is a model for enabling convenient, on-demand network access to a shared pool of configurable computing resources (e.g., networks, servers, storage, applications, and services) that can be rapidly provisioned and released with minimal management effort or service provider interaction." The full extended definition describes five essential characteristics, three service models, and four deployment models. This definition is available as SP 800-145, *A NIST Definition of Cloud Computing*.

The NIST cloud computing team has formulated a strategy for facilitating the development of high-quality cloud computing standards. The strategy, Standards Acceleration to Jumpstart Adoption of Cloud Computing (SAJACC), describes a process for formulating cloud computing use cases and for judging the extent to which cloud system interfaces can satisfy them. An output of the SAJACC program is a set of test results about the sufficiency of selected cloud interfaces (or parts of their interfaces); these results will help standards development organizations formulate their standards to achieve the central goals of portability, interoperability, and support for security. The SAJACC project is distributing results using a network-accessible portal that also serves as a communication focal point between NIST and the larger technical community. The cloud computing project has developed an initial set of 24 cloud system use cases, and has posted those use cases as working documents on the portal (http://www.nist.gov/itl/cloud).

In support of SAJACC, CSD built a heterogeneous virtualized environment to support some of the use cases by implementing a proof of concept for supporting the SP 800-53 security control requirements for low- and moderate-impact baseline to a cloud computing service model such as infrastructure as a service reference implementation; this includes typical virtual workloads running on commercial hypervisors. A typical use case involves migrating virtual workloads from a private cloud to a public or community cloud while demonstrating compliance with the security and audit requirements such as geographical location.

During FY2011, the cloud computing team, in collaboration with other NIST divisions, supported a large expansion of the scope of the NIST Cloud Computing Program. This extended scope included the formation of a NIST working group for the SAJACC effort; the formation of a NIST working group for studying security in cloud computing; the formation of a working group for standards in cloud computing; the initiation of the Federal Cloud Computing Standards and Technology Working Group; and the development of the U.S. Government Cloud Computing Technology Roadmap, which was released in November 2011.

During FY2011, the cloud computing team supported two Cloud Computing Forums held in Gaithersburg, Maryland, one in November 2010 and one in April 2011. As part of the SAJACC effort, the cloud computing team developed software implementations of six out of the 24 NIST technical cloud computing use cases; the implementations are available at: http://collaborate.nist.gov/twiki-cloud-computing/bin/view/CloudComputing/SAJACC. As part of the NIST standards working group effort, the cloud computing team contributed to Draft SP 500-291, *NIST Cloud Computing Standards Roadmap*. As part of the NIST security working group, the cloud computing team drafted the "Cloud Computing Security Impediments and Mitigations List"; this working document is available at: http://collaborate.nist.gov/twiki-cloud-computing/bin/view/CloudComputing/CloudSecurity. The cloud computing team furthermore developed two Draft SPs and one final SP. These publications are: Draft SP 800-144, *Guidelines on Security and Privacy in Public Cloud Computing* Draft SP 800-146, *Cloud Computing Synopsis and Recommendations*, and SP 800-145, *The NIST Definition of Cloud Computing*.

In FY2011, the cloud computing team also presented the findings and status of the cloud computing program in a variety of conferences and workshops.

The NIST cloud computing project is also supporting the cloud computing groups under the Federal CIO Council. This includes providing technical advice to the Cloud Computing Executive Steering Committee, the Cloud Computing Advisory Council, and the Information Security and Identity Management Committee's Web 2.0 working group.

http://www.nist.gov/itl/cloud
Contact:
   Mr. Lee Badger
   (301) 975-3176
   lee.badger@nist.gov

Security Ontologies for Risk Assessment

In the course of time, computer security has become a diversified field of research. It has become increasingly difficult for experts of different domains to understand each other and to use a precisely defined terminology. Therefore, there is a need for a security ontology that can clearly define security related concepts and their relationships, which can then be used to do quantitative risk analysis for enterprise information systems. The main goal of our research in this project is to develop an ontology that "knows" which threats endanger which assets and which security controls can reduce the probability of attacks. In addition each asset and each countermeasure in the ontology can be annotated with various types of cost and benefits. By comparing various scenarios during a quantitative risk analysis, organizations can choose

which security controls are more effective. The ontology will help to ensure a shared and accurate knowledge of threats and countermeasures, and will provide objective data for decision making about which countermeasures, if implemented, will be most effective.

In FY2011, we developed a security ontology that describes entities such as threats, vulnerabilities, countermeasures, assets and security objectives. We have implemented this ontology using Protégé and have a description of these entities in Resource Description Framework (RDF) and Web Ontology Language (OWL). In FY2012, we plan to develop graphical tools for a user to visualize ontologies and to generate reports about enterprise level security metrics.

Contact:
   Dr. Anoop Singhal
   (301) 975-4432
   anoop.singhal@nist.gov

Mobile Device Security

Smart phones have become both ubiquitous and indispensable for consumers and business people alike. Although these devices are relatively small and inexpensive, they can be used not only for voice calls and simple text messages, but also for many functions once limited to laptop and desktop computers. Smart phones and tablet devices have specialized built-in hardware, such as photographic cameras, video cameras, accelerometers, Global Positioning System (GPS) receivers, and removable-media readers. Furthermore, they employ a range of wireless interfaces, including infrared, Wireless Fidelity (Wi-Fi), Bluetooth, Near Field Communications (NFC), and one or more types of cellular interfaces that provide network connectivity across the globe. Although small in terms of form-factor, they can be used for sending and receiving email, browsing the web, online banking and commerce, social networking, storing and modifying documents, remotely accessing data, recording audio and video, and as navigation aids. Naturally, just as consumers and business people can realize productivity gains from these technologies, so can government agencies.

Like any new technology, smart phones present new capabilities, but also a number of new security challenges. Moreover, as the pace of the technology life cycles continues to increase, our current Information Assurance standards and processes must be updated and new technologies developed to transition from the use of specialized Government Off-The-Shelf (GOTS) products to Commercial Off-The-Shelf (COTS) products to allow government users to use the latest and greatest technologies that consumers can use without sacrificing any privacy and security.

NIST is working with Defense Advanced Research Projects Agency (DARPA) to develop open source FIPS-140-2 validated cryptographic algorithms, to develop new testing methodologies for smart phone software (apps), to provide updated security guidance for government users, and is working with industry to bridge the security gaps present on today's smart phones.

NIST analyzed Android apps using commercial and open source static analysis tools, designed an App Testing Portal (ATP), and implemented a proof-of-concept ATP. NIST worked closely with DARPA and the George Mason University to develop an encrypted file system using FIPS-140-2-validated open source cryptographic modules.

NIST will have a prototype smart phone app testing portal and associated documentation available at the end of FY2012. NIST will also publish updated guidance documents on smart phone security.

Contacts:

Dr. Steve Quirolgico
(301) 975-8426
stephen.quirolgico@nist.gov

Dr. Jeffrey Voas
(301) 975-6622
jeff.voas@nist.gov

Dr. Tom Karygiannis
301-975-4728
karygiannis@nist.gov

Access Control and Privilege Management

Access Control and Privilege Management Research

With the advance of current computing technologies and the multifaceted environments the technologies are applied to, security issues such as situation awareness, trust management, privacy control for access control, and privilege management systems are becoming more complex. However, the research available on these topics is generally targeted to a specific system, is incomplete, makes assumptions, or is ambiguous regarding critical elements. Thus, practical and conceptual general guidance for these topics is needed.

In FY2011, we investigated trust management frameworks and the situation awareness feature of access control mechanisms. We held two research seminars: *Automatic Extraction and Validation of Security Policies from Natural Language Documents* and *Government Open Source Access Control—Next Generation (GOSAC-N)*. We developed an evaluation metric for access control systems. The evaluation metric will define and describe access control properties, which will then be used in the metric as factors for the evaluation or comparison of access control

mechanisms/products. We worked on research of the unified enforcement technology for data services through Policy Machine (PM). During FY2011, we worked on a draft NIST Interagency Report (NISTIR) 7815, *Access Control for Suspicious Activity Report (SAR) Systems*, for the Policy Evaluation Testbed (PET) project, which enables the automatic privacy access control for Suspicious Activity Report systems. This draft NISTIR should be made publicly available sometime in the first half of FY2012.

In FY2012, we will complete the writing of a draft SP, *Guidelines for Access Control System Evaluation Metrics*; research unified enforcement mechanism of data services from Policy Machine (PM) for Enterprise Computing environment; enhance the capabilities of the Access Control Policy Tool (ACPT); and research algorithms for conflict resolution when combining and extending access control modes, rules, and policies.

We expect that this project will:

- Promote (or accelerate) the adoption of community computing that utilizes the power of shared resources and common trust management schemes;

- Provide a standard evaluation metric in evaluating or comparing access control mechanisms for implementing access control applications;

- Increase security and safety of static (connected) distributed systems by applying the testing and verification tool for the access control polices; and

- Assist system architects, security administrators, and security managers whose expertise is related to access control or privilege policy in managing their systems, and in learning the limitations and practical approaches for their applications.

Contacts:

Dr. Vincent Hu
(301) 975-4975
vhu@nist.gov

Mr. David Ferraiolo
(301) 975-3046
david.ferraiolo@nist.gov

Mr. Rick Kuhn
(301) 975-3337
kuhn@nist.gov

Conformance Verification for Access Control Policies

Access control systems are among the most critical network security components. Faulty policies, misconfigurations, or flaws in software implementation can result in serious vulnerabilities. The specification of access control policies is often a challenging problem. Often a system's privacy and security are compromised due to the misconfiguration of access control policies instead of the failure of cryptographic primitives or protocols. This problem becomes increasingly severe as software systems become more and more complex, and are deployed to manage a large amount of sensitive information and resources organized into sophisticated structures. Identifying discrepancies between policy specifications and their properties (intended function) is crucial because correct implementation and enforcement of policies by applications is based on the premise that the policy specifications are correct. As a result, policy specifications must undergo rigorous verification and validation through systematic testing to ensure that the policy specifications truly encapsulate the desires of the policy authors.

To formally and precisely capture the security properties that access control should adhere to, access control models are usually written to bridge the rather wide gap in abstraction between policy and mechanism. Thus, an access control model provides unambiguous and precise expression as well as reference for design and implementation of security requirements. Techniques are required for verifying whether an access control model is correctly expressed in the access controls policies and whether the properties are satisfied in the model. In practice, the same access control policies may express multiple access control models or express a single model in addition to extra access control constraints outside of the model. Ensuring the conformance of access control models and policies is a nontrivial and critical task.

Started in 2009, we developed a prototype system, Access Control Property Tool (ACPT), which allows a user to compose, verify, test, and generate access control policies.

During FY2011, in addition to continuing research, we enhanced the capability of ACPT by adding flexible states and classes for Workflow and Multilevel access control models, as well as performing Alpha and Beta testing for the tool. We also made ACPT available from the CSD website for public download.

In FY2012, we will continue Beta testing, enhance the capability of ACPT by adding new policy combine algorithms, apply more stringent and practical user cases to test ACPT's performance, and research an additional modeling method that is more flexible than the current one used. We will also produce a new user manual that contains examples and detail information of ACPT.

This project is expected to:

- Provide generic paradigm and framework of access control model/property conformance testing;
- Provide templates for specifying access control rules in popular access control models such as Attribute Based, Multilevel, and Workflow models;
- Provide tools or services for checking the security and safety of access control implementation, policy combination, and XACML policy generation;
- Promote (or accelerate) the adoption of combinatorial testing for large-system (such as access control system) testing; and
- Assist system architects, security administrators, and security managers whose expertise is related to access control in managing their systems, and to learn the limitations and practical approaches for their applications.

http://csrc.nist.gov/groups/SNS/acpt/
Contacts:

Dr. Vincent Hu	Mr. Rick Kuhn
(301) 975-4975	(301) 975-3337
vhu@nist.gov	kuhn@nist.gov

Metrics for Evaluation of Access Control Systems

Access control (AC) systems come with a wide variety of features and administrative capabilities, and the operational impact can be significant. In particular, this impact can pertain to administrative and user productivity, as well as to the organization's ability to perform its mission. Therefore, it is reasonable to use a quality metric to verify the mechanical properties of AC systems. Features that influence the development of this metric are: 1) administration is the main consideration of cost; 2) enforcement capabilities are the requirements for AC applications; 3) the performance is the major factor for the AC usability; and 4) support functions allow an AC system to utilize and connect to relate technologies so as to enable more efficient integration with network and host service functions. This project provides a metric for the evaluation of AC systems based on the features of administration, enforcement, performance, and support of AC properties.

The ability of an organization to enforce its access policies determines the degree to which its data may be protected and shared among its user community. The focus on sharing and protecting information is becoming increasingly acute for many organizations. Unfortunately, when it comes to AC systems, one size does not fit all. The quality of administrative capabilities has an impact on administrative cost, user downtime between administrative events, and the abilities of users to perform their duties, as well as the overall security posture of the enterprise. Currently no well-accepted metrics exist for measuring the effectiveness or functional quality of an AC system.

The purpose of this project is to provide federal agencies with background information on access control properties, and to help agencies improve the evaluation of their AC systems. This project provides information of the administration, enforcement, performance, and support properties of AC mechanisms that are embedded in each AC system. Properties discussed in this project extend to the information in NISTIR 7316, *Assessment of Access Control Systems*, which demonstrates the fundamental concept of policy, models, and mechanisms of AC systems.

In FY2011, we started working on a draft SP, *Guidelines for Access Control System Evaluation Metrics* (will be released during FY2012), which includes detailed items for AC system properties, as well as examples to demonstrate how to use the metric in evaluating and comparing capabilities for AC systems, which can be applied to application or research environments.

In FY2012, we will complete the writing of the SP, *Guidelines for Access Control System Evaluation Metrics*, and make it available for public comment. We will revise the document based on the research for more properties and items including those for the Privilege Management.

We expect that this project will:

- Provide detailed information on the evaluation of AC systems, including policies, models, and mechanism for AC system researchers;

- Help security policy makers and system administrators in planning and improving their current and extended future AC systems;

- Provide information for AC system developers in the consideration of architecture, requirements, and performance of an AC system; and

- Provide reference information for AC system-related standards.

Contacts:

Dr. Vincent Hu
(301) 975-4975
vhu@nist.gov

Mr. David Ferraiolo
(391) 975-3046
david.ferraiolo@nist.gov

Mr. Rick Kuhn
(301) 975-3337
kuhn@nist.gov

Policy Machine

In the early days of shared computing, access control and the policies it supports pertained to who could read and write what files - all within the confines of a single and largely isolated system. Since that period, however, computing has become increasingly distributed, and applications have simultaneously become sophisticated and interdependent. Today, policies need to be enforced within and across a multitude of heterogeneous file management systems, and across such applications as email, workflow, and records management. Associated with these data services are specific operations and resource types over which policy needs to be enforced. As such, policy enforcement today needs to contend with a large variety of operation types to include read/write, send, review, approve, insert, and copy/cut-paste. In addition, these operation types are applied to a large variety of data types such as files, messages, attachments, work items, records, fields, and clipboards. Further, these operations are performed under the control of a multitude of systems and applications often running simultaneously and with great interdependence.

The existing approach to access control and computing has been traditionally a source of great frustration on the part of users and administrators alike and source of serious security operational vulnerabilities. Administrators must mange a multitude of user accounts for each user, independently manage privileges, and attempt to coordinate access policy across different data services through different interfaces. Users must authenticate to a multitude of different data services in order to exercise legitimate capabilities, potentially through different authentication schemes. And, access control and other security mechanisms must be implemented within applications leading to greater exposure to attack and bypass.

The Policy Machine (PM) research effort is focused on solving these and other security issues. The PM is a redefinition of access control and data services in terms of what is believed to be their underlying elements, relations, and functions. The PM is a first step towards the notion of an "Enterprise Operating System." Through its configuration alone, the PM both enables the capabilities of a wide variety of data services and comprehensively enforces enterprise specific access control policies over user executions of those capabilities.

Although applicable to a variety of situations, the PM is ideal for rapid formation of ad hoc collaborations that emphasize sharing of sensitive data.

Although the PM is amenable to a verity of deployments, in FY2011 we began its implementation in a cloud/virtualized computing environment, where data services, users, data objects, and access control policies can be easily provisioned and managed in meeting the mission needs of the subscriber. It fills an important void with cloud computing. That is, it provides subscribers with a great deal of control in specifying access control policies that are comprehensively enforced over data services.

Also in FY2011, NIST and other members of an Ad Hoc International Committee for Information Technology Standards (INCITS) working group continued development of a three-part PM standard under the title of "Next Generation Access Control" (NGAC). This work was conducted under three sub-projects:

- Project 2193-D: Next Generation Access Control – Implementation Requirements, Protocols and API Definitions;

- Project 2194-D: Next Generation Access Control – Functional Architecture; and

- Project 2195-D: Next Generation Access Control - Generic Operations & Abstract Data Structures.

In the coming year, we anticipate conducting a demonstration of the Cloud PM implementation, and bringing parts of the NGAC proposed standard to ballot by INCITS.

We expect that this project will:

- Offer users capabilities of a variety of services achieved through configuration of PM data alone, such as file management, email, workflow, and forms and records management, rather than managing overlapping user accounts, and potentially different authentication schemes for each data service, through a single authenticated session;

- Deliver to select users, through the policy machine, select capabilities (of different services) under combinations of arbitrary, but mission-tailored forms of discretionary, mandatory, and history-based access controls, rather than deploying and managing different access control schemes for different data services;

- Provide an inherent property of the PM, the comprehensive nature in which data services interplay. For instance, a user can attach a record, created under a relational database management service, to an email message and send that record to any chosen individual. This property is not achieved through interoperability features, but rather through the underlying framework of the PM that inherently provides a foundational basis for interoperability; and

- Provide another inherent property of the PM, the comprehensive nature in which data is protected across data services. For example, regardless of the recipient of the message, any user who opens the attached record would only be able to read and/or write fields for which the user is authorized.

Contacts:

Mr. David Ferraiolo
(301) 975-3046
david.ferraiolo@nist.gov

Mr. Serban Gavrila
(301) 975-4343
serban.gavrila@nist.gov

Automated Vulnerability Management

Security Automation

Security automation harmonizes the vast amount of IT product data into coherent, comparable information streams to achieve situational awareness that informs timely and active management of diverse IT systems. Through the creation of flexible, open standards and international recognition, security automation will result in IT infrastructure interoperability, broad acceptance, and adoption, and will create opportunities for innovation.

Security Content Automation Protocol (SCAP)

To support the overarching security automation vision, it is necessary to have both trusted information and a standardized means to store and share it. Through close work with its government and industry partners, NIST has developed the Security Content Automation Protocol (SCAP) to provide the standardized technical mechanisms to share information between systems. Through the National Vulnerability Database (NVD) and the National Checklist Program (NCP), NIST is providing relevant and important information in the areas of vulnerability and configuration management. Combined, SCAP and the programs that leverage it are moving the information assurance industry towards being able to standardize communications, collect and store relevant data in standardized formats, and provide automated means for the assessment and remediation of systems for both vulnerabilities and configuration compliance.

SCAP is a suite of specifications that use eXtensible Markup Language (XML) to standardize the format and nomenclature by which security software products communicate information about software flaws and security configurations. SCAP includes software flaw and security configuration standard reference data, also known as SCAP content. This reference data is provided by the NVD (http://nvd.nist.gov/).

SCAP is a multipurpose protocol that supports automated vulnerability checking, technical control compliance activities, and security measurement. The U.S. government, in cooperation with academia and private industry, is adopting SCAP and encourages its use in support of security automation activities and initiatives.

At the end of September 2011, draft SP 800-126 Revision 2, *The Technical Specification for the Security Content Automation Protocol (SCAP): SCAP Version 1.2;*, was approved as final and is the SCAP technical specification (http://csrc.nist.gov/publications/nistpubs/800-126-rev2/SP800-126r2.pdf). This document describes the 11 component specifications comprising SCAP:

- Languages:

  - Extensible Configuration Checklist Description Format (XCCDF), a language for authoring security checklists/benchmarks and for reporting results of evaluating them;

  - Open Vulnerability and Assessment Language (OVAL), a language for representing system configuration information, assessing machine state, and reporting assessment results; and

  - Open Checklist Interactive Language (OCIL), a language for representing checks that collect information from people or from existing data stores made by other data collection efforts;

- Reporting Formats:

  - Asset Reporting Format (ARF), a format for expressing the transport format of information about assets and the relationships between assets and reports; and

  - Asset Identification (AI), a format for uniquely identifying assets based on known identifiers and/or known information about the assets;

- Enumerations:

  - Common Platform Enumeration (CPE), a nomenclature and dictionary of hardware, operating systems, and applications;

  - Common Configuration Enumeration (CCE), a nomenclature and dictionary of software security configurations; and

  - Common Vulnerabilities and Exposures (CVE), a nomenclature and dictionary of security-related software flaws;

- Mesurement and Scoring Systems:

  - Common Vulnerability Scoring System (CVSS), a specification for measuring the relative severity of software flaw vulnerabilities; and

  - Common Configuration Scoring System (CCSS), a specification for measuring the relative severity of system security configuration issues; and

- Integrity:

  - Trust Model for Security Automation Data (TMSAD), a specification for using digital signatures in a common trust model applied to security automation specifications.

SCAP is being widely adopted by major software and hardware manufacturers and has become a significant component of information security management and governance programs. The protocol is expected to evolve and expand in support of the growing need to define and measure effective security controls; assess and monitor ongoing aspects of information security; remediate noncompliance; and successfully manage systems in accordance with the Risk Management Framework described in SP 800-53, *Recommended Security Controls for Federal Information Systems and Organizations*, available at http://csrc.nist.gov/publications/.

Currently, CSD is leveraging SCAP in multiple areas, both to support our own mission and to enable other agencies and private sector entities to meet their goals. For CSD, SCAP is a critical component of the SCAP Validation Program, the NVD, and the National Checklist Program.

Contact:
Mr. Dave Waltermire
(301) 975-3390
david.waltermire@nist.gov

National Vulnerability Database (NVD)

The National Vulnerability Database (NVD) is the U.S. government repository of standards-based vulnerability management reference data. The NVD provides information regarding security vulnerabilities and configuration settings, vulnerability impact metrics, technical assessment methods, and references to remediation assistance and IT product identification data. The NVD reference data supports security automation efforts based on the Security Content Automation Protocol (SCAP). As of September 2011, the NVD contained the following resources:

- Over 47,000 vulnerability advisories with an average of 8 new vulnerabilities added daily;

- 36 SCAP-expressed checklists containing thousands of low-level security configuration checks that can be used by SCAP-validated security products to perform automated evaluations of system state;

- 159 non-SCAP security checklists (e.g., English prose guidance and configuration scripts);

- 212 U.S. Computer Emergency Readiness Team (US-CERT) alerts, 2,529 US-CERT vulnerability summaries, and 6,854 SCAP machine-readable software flaw checks;

- Product dictionary with 35,222 operating system, application, and hardware name entries; and

- 32,084 vulnerability advisories translated into Spanish.

NVD is sponsored by the Department of Homeland Security's National Cyber Security Division.

NVD's effective reach has been extended by the use of NVD SCAP data by commercial security products deployed in thousands of organizations worldwide. Increased adoption of SCAP is evidenced by the increasing demand for NVD XML data feeds and SCAP-expressed content from the NVD website. Concerted outreach efforts over the last year have resulted in an increase in the number of vendors providing SCAP-expressed content.

NVD continues to play a pivotal role in the payment card industry (PCI) efforts to mitigate vulnerabilities in credit card systems. PCI mandates the use of NVD vulnerability severity scores in measuring the risk to payment card servers worldwide and for prioritizing vulnerability patching. PCI's use of NVD severity scores helps enhance credit card transaction security and protects consumers' personal information.

Throughout FY2011, NVD continued to provide access to vulnerability reference data and security checklists. NVD deployed an enhanced checklist submission web interface and a web service checklist submission capability. Additionally, the NVD now hosts a SCAP Content Validation Tool that can be used by creators of SCAP content to ensure that their SCAP content packages conform to SP 800-126, *The Technical Specification for the Security Content Automation Protocol (SCAP): SCAP Version 1.2*, guidelines. Finally, NVD now supports automated SCAP content generation from the Common Vulnerabilities and Exposures (CVE) vulnerability data feed. NVD data is a fundamental component of our security automation infrastructure and is substantially increasing the security of networks worldwide. CSD plans to expand and improve the NVD in FY2012.

http://nvd.nist.gov
Contacts:

Mr. John Banghart
(301) 975-8514
john.banghart@nist.gov

Mr. Harold Booth
(301) 975-8441
harold.booth@nist.gov

National Checklist Program

There are many threats to information technology (IT), ranging from remotely launched network service exploits to malicious code spread through infected emails, websites, and downloaded files. Vulnerabilities in IT products are discovered daily, and many ready-to-use exploitation techniques are widely available on the Internet. Because IT products are often intended for a wide variety of audiences, restrictive security configuration controls are usually not enabled by default. As a result, many out-of-the-box IT products are immediately vulnerable. In addition, identifying a reasonable set of security settings that achieve balanced risk management is a complicated, arduous, and time-consuming task, even for experienced system administrators.

To facilitate development of security configuration checklists for IT products and to make checklists more organized and usable, NIST established the National Checklist Program (NCP) in furtherance of its statutory responsibilities under the Federal Information Security Management Act (FISMA) of 2002, Public Law 107-347, and also under the Cyber Security Act, which tasks NIST to "develop, and revise as necessary, a checklist setting forth settings and option selections that minimize the security risks associated with each computer hardware or software system that is, or is likely to become widely used within the federal government." In February 2008, revised Part 39 of the Federal Acquisition Regulation (FAR) was published. Paragraph (d) of section 39.101 states, "In acquiring information technology, agencies shall include the appropriate IT security policies and requirements, including use of common security configurations available from the NIST website at http://checklists.nist.gov. Agency contracting officers should consult with the requiring official to ensure the appropriate standards are incorporated." In Memorandum M08-22, Office of Management and Budget (OMB) mandated the use of SCAP-validated products for continuous monitoring of Federal Desktop Core Configuration (FDCC) compliance. The NCP strives to encourage and make simple agencies' compliance with these mandates.

The goals of the NCP are to:

- Facilitate development and sharing of checklists by providing a formal framework for checklist developers to submit checklists to NIST;

- Provide guidance to developers to help them create standardized, high-quality checklists that conform to common operations environments;

- Help developers and users by providing guidelines for making checklists better documented and more usable;

- Encourage software vendors and other parties to develop checklists;

- Provide a managed process for the review, update, and maintenance of checklists;

- Provide an easy-to-use repository of checklists; and,

- Encourage the use of automation technologies for checklist application such as SCAP.

There are 195 checklists posted on the website; 36 of the checklists are SCAP-expressed (see section on SCAP above) and can be used with SCAP-validated products. It is anticipated that a minimum of several more SCAP-expressed checklists will be added in FY2012 as contributions come from other federal agencies and product vendors. Organizations can use checklists obtained from the NCP website (http://checklists.nist.gov) for automated security configuration patch assessment. NCP currently hosts SCAP checklists for Internet Explorer 7.0, Internet Explorer 8.0, Office 2007, Red Hat Enterprise Linux, Windows 7, Windows Vista, Windows XP, and other products.

To assist users in identifying automated checklist content, NCP groups checklists into tiers, from Tier I to Tier IV. NCP uses the tiers to rank checklists according to their automation capability. Tier III and IV checklists are considered production-ready and have been validated by the SCAP content validation tool as conforming to the requirements outlined in SP 800-126, *The Technical Specification for the Security Content Automation Protocol (SCAP)*. Tier IV checklists are used in the SCAP Validation Program (see following section for details) when validating SCAP products. Tier III checklists are not presently used in the SCAP Validation Program; however, Tier III checklists should be compatible with SCAP-validated products. Tier II checklists document recommended security settings in a machine-readable, nonstandard format, such as a proprietary format or a product-specific configuration script. Tier I checklists are prose-based and contain no machine-readable content. Users can browse the checklists based on the checklist tier, IT product, IT product category, or authority, and also through a keyword search that searches the checklist name and summary for user-specified terms. The search results show the detailed checklist metadata and a link to any SCAP content for the checklist, as well as links to any supporting resources associated with the checklist.

The NCP is defined in SP 800-70 Revision 2, *National Checklist Program for IT Products—Guidelines for Checklist Users and Developers*, which can be found at http://csrc.nist.gov/publications/.

http://checklists.nist.gov
Contact:
Mr. Stephen Quinn
(301) 975-6967
stephen.quinn@nist.gov

Security Content Automation Protocol (SCAP) Validation Program

The SCAP Validation Program performs conformance testing to ensure that products correctly implement SCAP as defined in SP 800-126. Conformance testing is necessary because SCAP is a complex specification consisting of eleven individual specifications that work together to meet various use cases. A single error in product implementation could result in undetected vulnerabilities or policy noncompliance within agency and industry networks.

The SCAP Validation Program was created by request of the OMB to support the Federal Desktop Core Configuration (FDCC) and United States Government Configuration Baseline (USGCB). The program coordinates its work with the NIST National Voluntary Laboratory Accreditation Program (NVLAP) to set up independent conformance testing laboratories that conduct the testing based on draft NISTIR 7511 Revision 3, *Security Content Automation Protocol (SCAP) Version 1.2 Validation Program Test Requirements*. When testing is completed, the laboratory submits a test report to CSD for review and approval. SCAP validation testing has been designed to be inexpensive, yet effective. The SCAP conformance tests are either easily human-verifiable or automated through NIST-provided reference tools. To date, the program has eight accredited independent laboratories and has validated 43 products from 32 different vendors.

The SCAP Validation Program will expand in FY2012 to include additional capabilities, provide enhanced testing support, and evolve to include new technologies as SCAP itself matures. Current expansion includes support for the U.S. Government Configuration Baseline initiative, which plans to release configuration baselines for Microsoft Windows 7/IE8 and Red Hat Enterprise Linux 5.

http://scap.nist.gov/validation/
Contact:
Mr. John Banghart
(301) 975-8514
john.banghart@nist.gov

Technical Security Metrics

Measurement is the key to making major advancements in any scientific field, and computer security is no exception. Measures give us a standardized way of expressing and quantifying security characteristics. Because of the ever-increasing complexity of threats, vulnerabilities, and mitigation strategies, there is a particularly strong need for additional research on attack, vulnerability, and security control measurements. Improved measurement capabilities in these areas would allow organizations to make scientifically sound decisions when planning, implementing, and configuring security controls. This would improve the effectiveness of security controls, while reducing costs by eliminating unnecessary and ineffective controls. In FY2011, CSD continued its long-term research efforts on technical security metrics. The first stage of this work involved developing specifications for measuring and scoring individual vulnerabilities and configurations, and researching how vulnerabilities from multiple hosts can be used in sequence to compromise particular targets. A summary of these efforts from the past year is presented below.

Vulnerability Measurement and Scoring

The Common Vulnerability Scoring System (CVSS) is an industry standard that enables the security community to calculate the relative severity of software flaw vulnerabilities within information technology systems through sets of security metrics and formulas. During the past year, NIST security staff continued to provide technical leadership in determining how CVSS could be adapted for use with other types of vulnerabilities besides software flaws. This work has involved evaluating and refining the following draft specifications:

The Common Configuration Scoring System (CCSS), which was originally proposed in draft NISTIR 7502, *The Common Configuration Scoring System (CCSS): Metrics for Software Security Configuration Vulnerabilities*. CCSS is based on CVSS and the Common Misuse Scoring System (CMSS) but has been customized for use with software security configuration-related vulnerabilities.

This completes the first stage of CSD's technical security metrics research. The second stage of the work is expected to involve supporting the implementation of these specifications, such as creating standardized reference data for CCSS, and researching how these specifications can be used together to better conceptualize and quantify the security posture of systems.

Contact:
Mr. John Banghart
(301) 975-8514
john.banghart@nist.gov

Security Risk Analysis of Enterprise Networks Using Attack Graphs

At present, computer networks constitute the core component of information technology infrastructures in areas such as power grids, financial data systems, and emergency communication systems. Protection of these networks from malicious intrusions is critical to the economy and security of our nation. Vulnerabilities are regularly discovered in software applications which are exploited to stage cyber attacks. Currently, management of security risk of an enterprise network is more an art than a science. System administrators operate by instinct and experience rather than relying on objective metrics to guide and justify decision making. The objective of this research is to develop a standard model for measuring security of computer networks. A standard model will enable us to answer questions such as "Are we more secure now than yesterday?" or "How does the security of one network configuration compare with another one?" Also, having a standard model to measure network security will allow users, vendors, and researchers to evaluate methodologies and products for network security in a coherent and consistent manner.

CSD has approached the challenge of network security analysis by capturing vulnerability interdependencies and measuring security in the exact way that real attackers penetrate the network. Our methodology for security risk analysis is based on the model of attack graphs. We analyze all attack paths through a network, providing a probabilistic metric of the overall system risk. Through this metric, we analyze trade-offs between security costs and security benefits.

In FY2011, we worked on validating our approach for realistic networks. We used a real network as a test bed to demonstrate the utility of this approach. The results of our experiments were published as a paper "An Empirical Study of Vulnerability Aggregation Method" in proceedings of the 2011 World Congress in Computer Science, Special Track on Security and Mission Assurance. In FY2012, we plan to integrate our techniques into existing attack graph-based security tools. We also plan to publish our results as a NIST report and as a paper in conferences and journals.

http://csrc.nist.gov/groups/SNS/security-risk-analysis-enterprise-networks/
Contact:
Dr. Anoop Singhal
(301) 975-4432
anoop.singhal@nist.gov

Infrastructure Services, Protocols, and Applications

Internet Protocol Version 6 (IPv6) and Internet Protocol Security (IPsec)

Internet Protocol Version 6 (IPv6) is an updated version of the current Internet Protocol, IPv4. The primary motivations for the development of IPv6 were to increase the number of unique IP addresses and to handle the needs of new Internet applications and devices. In addition, IPv6 was designed with the following goals: increased ease of network management and configuration; expandable IP headers; improved mobility and security; and quality of service controls. IPv6 has been, and continues to be, developed and defined by the Internet Engineering Task Force (IETF).

This year was a significant year for the deployment of IPv6. In January 2011, the Internet Assigned Numbers Authority (IANA) distributed the last five blocks of globally unique IPv4 addresses to the five Regional Internet Registries (RIRs). Once these IPv4 addresses are assigned for use, any organizations needing additional global IP addresses will be required to use IPv6.

The NIST IPv6 Test Program, whose goal is to provide assurance on IPv6 conformance and interoperability of products, continued to operate. Additional tests were added: the Supplier's Declaration of Conformity (SDOC), the vehicle used to enable vendors of IPv6 products to report the details of their products that have successfully executed the United States Government IPv6 (USGv6) tests, was improved, and a draft version of the USGv6 Buyers' Guide was published.

SP 800-119, *Guidelines for the Secure Deployment of IPv6*, was published in FY2011. This document describes and analyzes the numerous protocols that comprise IPv6, including addressing, domain name system (DNS), routing, mobility, quality of service, multihoming, IPsec, etc. For each component, there is a detailed analysis of the differences between IPv4 and IPv6, the security ramifications, and any unknown aspects. It characterizes new security threats posed by the transition to IPv6 and provides guidelines on IPv6 deployment, including transition, integration, configuration, and testing. It also addresses more recent significant changes in the approach to IPv6 transition.

As a result of both the IPv4 address depletion and the publication of SP 800-119, *Guidelines for the Secure Deployment of IPv6*, NIST personnel were in demand for interviews (press and radio) and also for presentations on IPv6 deployment and security (including the First IPv6 World Congress, the Fourth Annual IPv6 Technology Conference, the Information Systems Security Association, and numerous others).

In FY2012, NIST will continue to manage and evolve the USGv6 Test Program; the NIST IPv6 Profile will also be updated.

---

http://www.antd.nist.gov/usgv6
Contacts:

Ms. Sheila Frankel	Mr. Douglas Montgomery
(301) 975-3297	(301) 975-3630
sheila.frankel@nist.gov	dougm@nist.gov

Securing the Domain Name System (DNS)

The Domain Name System (DNS) is a global distributed system in which Internet addresses in mnemonic form, such as http://csrc.nist.gov; are converted into the equivalent numeric Internet Protocol (IP) addresses such as 129.6.13.39. Certain servers throughout the world maintain the databases needed, as well as perform the translations. A DNS server that is performing a translation may communicate with other Internet DNS servers if it does not have the data needed to translate the address itself.

As with other Internet-based systems, DNS is subject to several threats. To counter these threats, the Internet Engineering Task Force (IETF) developed a set of specifications for securing DNS called DNS Security Extensions (DNSSEC) to provide origin authentication and data integrity for all responses from the DNS. In partnership with the Department of Homeland (DHS) Security, NIST has been actively involved in promoting the deployment of DNSSEC since 2004.

The significant achievements in FY2011 are as follows:

- Co-Chaired the DNSSEC and Email Authentication Tiger Team set up by DHS and the Federal CIO Council. The goal of the Tiger Team was to promote DNSSEC deployment and work on a process of continuous monitoring of DNS health within the .gov;

- Worked with GSA on developing new policy for the .gov top-level domain (TLD);

- Continued the Secure Naming Infrastructure Pilot (SNIP) operations in 2011. The SNIP is a distributed test bed to help U.S. Government DNS administrators deploy DNSSEC and test new DNSSEC implementations. The new SNIP monitor incorporates other DNSSEC scanner technologies (DNSViz) for error visualization for administrators; and

- Hosted a session in FOSE 2011 consisting of presentations and question and answer sessions for assisting agencies with DNSSEC deployments.

Contacts:

Dr. Ramaswamy Chandramouli
(301) 975-5013
mouli@nist.gov

Mr. Scott Rose
(301) 975-8439
scott.rose@nist.gov

CSD's Part in National and International ISO Security Standards Processes

Figure 1 below shows the many national and international standards-developing organizations (SDOs) involved in cybersecurity standardization. NIST CSD staff participates in many cybersecurity standards activities in many of these organizations, either in leadership positions or as editors and contributors. Many of CSD's publications have been the basis for both national and international standards projects. This section of the annual report primarily concerns CSD standards activities in conjunction with INCITS Technical Committee CS1, where Dan Benigni serves as Chair and U.S. Head of Delegation to SC 27.

The International Organization for Standardization

The International Organization for Standardization (ISO) is a network of the national standards institutes of 148 countries, with the representation of one member per country. The scope of ISO covers standardization in all fields except electrical and electronic engineering standards, which are the responsibility of the International Electrotechnical Commission (IEC).

The IEC prepares and publishes international standards for all electrical, electronic, and related technologies, including electronics, magnetics and electromagnetics, electroacoustics, multimedia, telecommunication, and energy production and distribution, as well as associated general disciplines such as terminology and symbols, electromagnetic compatibility, measurement and performance, dependability, design and development, safety, and the environment.

Joint Technical Committee 1 (JTC1) was formed by ISO and IEC to be responsible for international standardization in the field of Information Technology. It develops, maintains, promotes, and facilitates IT standards required by global markets, meeting business and user requirements concerning—

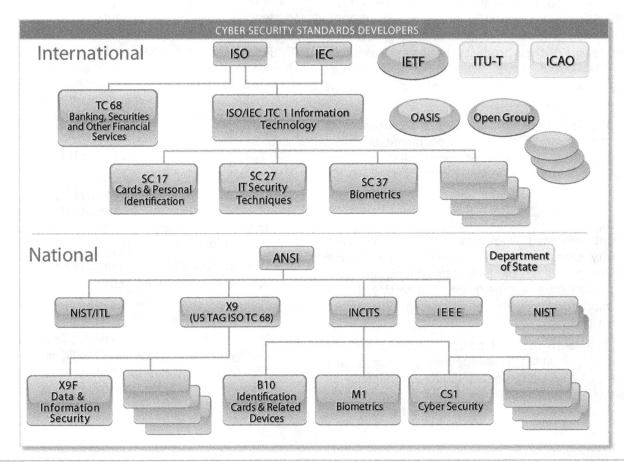

- Design and development of IT systems and tools;
- Performance and quality of IT products and systems;
- Security of IT systems and information;
- Portability of application programs;
- Interoperability of IT products and systems;
- Unified tools and environments;
- Harmonized IT vocabulary; and
- User-friendly and ergonomically designed user interfaces.

JTC1 consists of a number of subcommittees (SCs) and working groups that address specific technologies. SCs that produce standards relating to IT security include:

- SC 06 - Telecommunications and Information Exchange Between Systems;
- SC 17 - Cards and Personal Identification;
- SC 27 - IT Security Techniques; and
- SC 37 - Biometrics (Fernando Podio of NIST serves as Chair).

JTC1 also has—

- Technical Committee 68 - Financial Services;
- SC 2 - Operations and Procedures including Security;
- SC 4 - Securities;
- SC 6 - Financial Transaction Cards, Related Media and Operations; and
- SC 7 - Software and Systems Engineering.

The American National Standards Institute

The American National Standards Institute (ANSI) is a private, nonprofit organization (501(c)(3)) that administers and coordinates the U.S. voluntary standardization and conformity assessment system.

ANSI facilitates the development of American National Standards (ANSs) by accrediting the procedures of standards-developing organizations (SDOs). The InterNational Committee for Information Technology Standards (INCITS) is accredited by ANSI.

ANSI promotes the use of U.S. standards internationally, advocates U.S. policy and technical positions in international and regional standards organizations, and encourages the adoption of international standards as national standards where they meet the needs of the user community.

ANSI is the sole U.S. representative and dues-paying member of the two major non-treaty international standards organizations, ISO and, via the United States National Committee (USNC), the IEC.

INCITS serves as the ANSI Technical Advisory Group (TAG) for ISO/IEC Joint Technical Committee 1. INCITS is sponsored by the Information Technology Industry (ITI) Council, a trade association representing the leading U.S. providers of information technology products and services. INCITS currently has more than 800 published standards.

INCITS is organized into Technical Committees that focus on the creation of standards for different technology areas. Technical committees that focus on IT security and IT security-related technologies, or may require separate security standards include:

- B10 - Identification Cards and Related Devices (Sal Francomacaro chairs Task Group B10.12, Integrated Circuit Cards with Contacts);
- CS1 - Cyber Security (Dan Benigni, Chair and Richard Kissel, NIST Principal voting member);
- E22 - Item Authentication;
- M1 - Biometrics (Fernando Podio, Chair);
- T3 - Open Distributed Processing (ODP);
- T6 - Radio Frequency Identification (RFID) Technology;
- CGIT1 - Corporate Governance of IT (Richard Kissel, NIST Principal voting member and International Representative); and
- DAPS38 - Distributed Application Platforms and Services.

As a technical committee of INCITS, CS1 develops United States, national, ANSI-accredited standards in the area of cybersecurity. Its scope encompasses—

- Management of information security and systems;
- Management of third-party information security service providers;
- Intrusion detection;
- Network security;
- Incident handling;
- IT security evaluation and assurance;
- Security assessment of operational systems;
- Security requirements for cryptographic modules;
- Protection profiles;
- Role-based access control;
- Security checklists;

- Security metrics;
- Cryptographic and non-cryptographic techniques and mechanisms including:
  - confidentiality,
  - entity authentication,
  - non-repudiation,
  - key management,
  - data integrity,
  - message authentication,
  - hash functions, and
  - digital signatures;
- Future service and applications standards supporting the implementation of control objectives and controls as defined in ISO 27001, in the areas of—
  - business continuity, and
  - outsourcing;
- Identity management, including:
  - identity management framework,
  - role-based access control, and
  - single sign-on;
- Privacy technologies, including:
  - privacy framework,
  - privacy reference architecture,
  - privacy infrastructure,
  - anonymity and credentials, and
  - specific privacy-enhancing technologies.

The scope of CS1 explicitly excludes the areas of work on cybersecurity standardization presently under way in INCITS B10, M1, T3, T10 and T11, as well as other standard groups, such as the Alliance for Telecommunications Industry Solutions, the Institute of Electrical and Electronics Engineers, Inc., the Internet Engineering Task Force, the Travel Industry Association of America, and Accredited Standards Committee (ASC) X9. The CS1 scope of work includes standardization in most of the same cybersecurity areas as are covered in the NIST CSD.

As the U.S. TAG to ISO/IEC JTC 1/SC 27, CS1 contributes to the SC 27 program of work on IT Security Techniques in terms of comments and contributions on SC 27 standards projects; votes on SC 27 standards documents at various stages of development; and identifies U.S. experts to work on various SC 27 projects or to serve in various SC 27 leadership positions. Currently a number of CS1 members are serving as SC 27 document editors or co-editors on various standards projects, including Randy Easter, Erika McCallister, and Richard Kissel (all of NIST).

All input from CS1 is processed through INCITS to ANSI, then to SC 27. It is also a conduit for getting U.S.-based new work item proposals and U.S.-developed national standards into the international SC 27 standards development process. In its international efforts, CS1 has consistently, efficiently, and in a timely manner responded to all calls for contributions on all international security standards projects in ISO/IEC JTC1 SC 27.

Through its membership on CS1, where Dan Benigni serves as the nonvoting chair and Richard Kissel is the NIST Principal voting member, NIST contributes to many of CS1's national and international IT security standards efforts. Internationally, there are over 90 published standards, and almost all have been adopted as U.S. national standards. There are more than 85 current international standards projects.

CSD's Role in Cybersecurity Standardization

CSD's cybersecurity research also plays a direct role in the Cybersecurity Standardization efforts of CS1 at the national level. During FY2011:

1. The CS1 Task Group CS1.1 Role-Based Access Control (RBAC) published the national standard titled "Requirements for the Implementation and Interoperability of Role Based Access Control." In addition, the task group started work on the revision of INCITS 359 – 2004, "Role Based Access Control (RBAC)," as well as INCITS Project: 2215-D, "Information technology -- Role Based Access Control – Policy Enhanced" and Project 2214-D, "Process for Defining Roles for Role Based Access Control." NIST originally authored RBAC, and Rick Kuhn is the NIST Principal voting member.

2. The NIST Policy Machine research and development has resulted in three ongoing national standards projects in CS1 in the early stages of development. They include:

   a. Next Generation Access Control - Implementation Requirements, Protocols and API Definitions (NGAC-IRPADS). Its assigned project number is 2193-D, and Roger Cummings of Symantec is the editor;

   b. Next Generation Access Control - Functional Architecture (NGAC-FA). Its assigned project number is 2194-D, and David Ferraiolo of NIST is the editor; and

c. Next Generation Access Control - Generic Operations & Abstract Data Structures (NGAC-GOADS). Its assigned project number is 2195-D, and Serban Gavrila of NIST is the editor.

Within CS1, liaisons are maintained with nearly 20 organizations. They include the following:

- Open Group;
- IEEE P1700 and P1619;
- Forum of Incident Response and Security Teams (FIRST);
- American Bar Association (ABA), section on Science and Technology;
- ABA Federated Identity Management Legal (IdM Legal) Task Force;
- INCITS T11, M1, CGIT1, DAPS38 and PL22;
- Financial Services Technology Consortium (FSTC);
- Internet Security Alliance;
- Trusted Computing Group;
- Kantara Initiative Identity Assurance Working Group (IAWG);
- Cloud Computing Alliance;
- SC 7 TAG;
- Scientific Working Group on Digital Evidence (SWGDE);
- ITU-T Q4/17 and Q10/17; and
- The Storage Networking Industry Association (SNIA).

In FY2012, Dan Benigni will be the standards coordinator in CSD's division office.

Contact:
Mr. Daniel Benigni
(301) 975-3279
benigni@nist.gov

Department of Commerce Gold Medal

Marianne Swanson, CSD, and;

Nada Golmie (Advanced Network

Technologies Division [ANTD], ITL)

Citation: For developing a globally recognized Smart Grid standards framework enabling transition to a clean energy economy and increased United States competitiveness.

Top Ten Government Infosec Leaders in 2011

Marianne Swanson

GovInfoSecurity.com Top Ten Government Infosec Leaders in 2011. The award spotlights the most influential people in government cybersecurity for 2011. Those on the list contain a combination of position and know-how and demonstrated the ability to lead and collaborate. This year's winners also consisted of a few behind-the-scenes individuals who aren't as well known as others on the list, but have enormous sway in the government cybersecurity.

Department of Commerce Gold Medal

William (Tim) Polk, CSD;

Scott Rose and Douglas Montgomery both from ANTD, ITL

Citation: For the successful deployment of DNSSEC at the authoritative root zone that mitigates fundamental vulnerabilities and secures the Internet DNS.

InterNational Committee for Information Technology Standards Award

Fernando Podio

Fernando received the InterNational Committee for Information Technology Standards (INCITS) Award for Exceptional International Leadership for 2011 in recognition of numerous contributions to INCITS M1 and JTC 1/SC 37 and for having "proved to be an effective leader and diplomat in the domestic and international biometrics standardization activities."

Federal 100 Award Winner

Donna Dodson

The Federal 100 Awards program recognized Donna Dodson, Chief of the Computer Security Division, for her leadership skills and her untiring efforts to improve the secure implementation, management and use of information technology (IT) by the federal government. The Federal 100 recognize government and industry leaders who have played pivotal roles in the federal government IT community and who have gone above and beyond their daily responsibilities to make a difference and to affect change. The winners are nominated by readers of Federal Computer Week and selected by an independent panel of judges.

Donna's creativity and her ability to work with members of the White House staff, intelligence agencies and industry on cybersecurity helped to bring these diverse communities together, and to use NIST's security policies, best practices and tools more effectively. She was cited as one of the most trusted government advisers on cybersecurity.

INCITS Service Award for 2011

Dan Benigni

INCITS would like to recognize Dan Benigni's many contributions. As INCITS/CS1 Chairman, his management skills and willingness to accept responsibilities are one of the major contributing factors for the successful and timely development of standards nationally and internationally within ISO/IEC JTC 1/SC 27. Dan's knowledge and dedication on important issues reflect his commitment to standardization efforts. Without question, Dan Benigni has earned this award, and INCITS would like to recognize his contributions to INCITS.

Federal CIO 50 Award

Dr. Ron Ross

The *InformationWeek* Federal CIO 50 Award recognizes a select number of individuals within federal, state, and local government based on their technology vision, influence among peers in other agencies, and an ability to show tangible, measurable results in the field of information technology.

V. Lee Conyers Award

Dr. Ron Ross

The V. Lee Conyers Award was created by the ISACA®-National Capital Area Chapter (NCAC-ISACA) to honor and remember V. Lee Conyers, a distinguished member of the chapter. The award recognizes an outstanding chapter member in the field of IT Audit, Security, and Control.

Key to Publications:
FIPS = Federal Information Processing Standards
SPs = Special Publications
NISTIRs = NIST Interagency Reports
ITL = Information Technology Laboratory

DRAFT PUBLICATIONS

Type & Number	Publication Title	Draft Released Date	Finalized in FY2011? If Yes, date final was released
FIPS 201-2	Personal Identity Verification of Federal Employees and Contractors	March 2011	No
FIPS 180-4	Secure Hash Standard (SHS)	February 2011	No
SP 800-153	Guidelines for Securing Wireless Local Area Networks (WLANs)	September 2011	No
SP 800-147	BIOS Protection Guidelines	February 2011	Yes = April 2011
SP 800-146	Cloud Computing Synopsis and Recommendations	May 2011	No
SP 800-145	A NIST Definition of Cloud Computing	January 2011	Yes = September 2011
SP 800-144	Guidelines on Security and Privacy in Public Cloud Computing	January 2011	No
SP 800-133	Recommendations for Cryptographic Key Generation	August 2011	No
SP 800-131B	Transitions: Validation of Transitioning Cryptographic Algorithm and Key Lengths	February 2011	No
SP 800-131C	Transitions: Validating the Transition from FIPS 186-2 to FIPS 186-3	February 2011	No
SP 800-126 Revision 2	The Technical Specification for the Security Content Automation Protocol (SCAP): SCAP Version 1.2	July 2011	Yes = September 2011
SP 800-121 Revision 1	Guide to Bluetooth Security	September 2011	No
SP 800-107 Revision 1	Recommendation for Applications Using Approved Hash Algorithms	September 2011	No
SP 800-90A	Recommendation for Random Number Generation Using Deterministic Random Bit Generators	May 2011	No
SP 800-76-2	Biometric Data Specification for Personal Identity Verification	April 2011	No
SP 800-67 Revision 1	Recommendation for the Triple Data Encryption Algorithm (TDEA) Block Cipher	July 2011	No
SP 800-63 Revision 1 (Third Draft)	Electronic Authentication Guideline	June 2011	No
SP 800-57 Part 1	Recommendation for Key Management: Part 1: General	May 2011	No
SP 800-56C (Second Draft)	Recommendation for Key Derivation through Extraction-then-Expansion	July 2011	No
SP 800-53 Appendix J	Privacy Control Catalog	July 2011	No
SP 800-38F	Recommendation for Block Cipher Modes of Operation: Methods for Key Wrapping	August 2011	No
SP 800-30 Revision 1	Guide for Conducting Risk Assessments	September 2011	No
NISTIR 7802	Trust Model for Security Automation Data (TMSAD) Version 1.0	July 2011	Yes = September 2011
NISTIR 7756	CAESARS Framework Extension: An Enterprise Continuous Monitoring Technical Reference Architecture	February 2011	No
NISTIR 7698	Common Platform Enumeration: Applicability Language Specification Version 2.3	June 2011	Yes = August 2011
NISTIR 7697	Common Platform Enumeration: Dictionary Specification Version 2.3	June 2011	Yes = August 2011
NISTIR 7696	Common Platform Enumeration: Name Matching Specification Version 2.3	April 2011	Yes = August 2011

DRAFT PUBLICATIONS

Type & Number	Publication Title	Draft Released Date	Finalized in FY2011? If Yes, date final was released
NISTIR 7695	Common Platform Enumeration: Naming Specification Version 2.3	April 2011	Yes = August 2011
NISTIR 7670	Proposed Open Specifications for an Enterprise Remediation Automation Framework	February 2011	No
NISTIR 7511 Revision 2	Security Content Automation Protocol (SCAP) Version 1.0 Validation Program Test Requirements	February 2011	No
NISTIR 7275 Revision 4	Specification for the Extensible Configuration Checklist Description Format (XCCDF) Version 1.2	July 2011	Yes = September 2011

FEDERAL INFORMATION PROCESSING STANDARDS (FIPS)

None: There were no final approved FIPS during FY2011.

SPECIAL PUBLICATIONS (SPs)

SP Number	Title	Approval Date
SP 800-147	Basic Input/Output System (BIOS) Protection Guidelines	April 2011
SP 800-145	The NIST Definition of Cloud Computing	September 2011
SP 800-142	Practical Combinatorial Testing	October 2010
SP 800-137	Information Security Continuous Monitoring (ISCM) for Federal Information Systems and Organizations	September 2011
SP 800-135	Recommendation for Existing Application-Specific Key Derivation Functions	December 2010
SP 800-132	Recommendation for Password-Based Key Derivation Part 1: Storage Applications	December 2010
SP 800-131 A	Transitions: Recommendation for Transitioning the Use of Cryptographic Algorithms and Key Lengths	January 2011
SP 800-128	Guide for Security-Focused Configuration Management of Information Systems	August 2011
SP 800-126 Revision 2	The Technical Specification for the Security Content Automation Protocol (SCAP): SCAP Version 1.2	September 2011
SP 800-126 Revision 1	The Technical Specification for the Security Content Automation Protocol (SCAP): SCAP Version 1.1	February 2011
SP 800-125	Guide to Security for Full Virtualization Technologies	January 2011
SP 800-119	Guidelines for the Secure Deployment of IPv6	December 2010
SP 800-82	Guide to Industrial Control Systems (ICS) Security	June 2011
SP 800-78-3	Cryptographic Algorithms and Key Sizes for Personal Identity Verification	December 2010
SP 800-70 Revision 2	National Checklist Program for IT Products Guidelines for Checklist Users and Developers	February 2011
SP 800-51 Revision 1	Guide to Using Vulnerability Naming Schemes	February 2011
SP 800-39	Managing Information Security Risk: Organization, Mission, and Information System View	February 2011
SP 800-38 A - Addendum	Recommendation for Block Cipher Modes of Operation: Three Variants of Ciphertext Stealing for CBC Mode	October 2010

NIST INTERAGENCY REPORTS (NISTIRS)

NIST IR Number	Title	Approval Date
NISTIR 7806	ANSI/NIST-ITL 1-2011 Requirements and Conformance Test Assertions	September 2011
NISTIR 7802	Trust Model for Security Automation Data (TMSAD) Version 1.0	September 2011
NISTIR 7791	Conformance Test Architecture and Test Suite for ANSI/NIST-ITL 1-2007	June 2011

NIST INTERAGENCY REPORTS (NISTIRS)

NIST IR Number	Title	Approval Date
NISTIR 7773	ANSI/NIST-ITL 1-2011 Requirements and Conformance Test Assertions	February 2011
NISTIR 7771	Conformance Test Architecture for Biometric Data Interchange Formats - Version Beta 2.0	March 2011
NISTIR 7770	Security Considerations for Remote Electronic UOCAVA Voting	February 2011
NISTIR 7764	Status Report on the Second Round of the SHA-3 Cryptographic Hash Algorithm Competition	February 2011
NISTIR 7751	2010 Annual Report, Computer Security Division	May 2011
NISTIR 7711	Security Best Practices for the Electronic Transmission of Election Materials for UOCAVA Voters	August 2011
NISTIR 7698	Common Platform Enumeration: Applicability Language Specification Version 2.3	August 2011
NISTIR 7697	Common Platform Enumeration: Dictionary Specification Version 2.3	August 2011
NISTIR 7696	Common Platform Enumeration: Name Matching Specification Version 2.3	August 2011
NISTIR 7695	Common Platform Enumeration: Naming Specification Version 2.3	August 2011
NISTIR 7694	Specification for the Asset Reporting Format 1.1	June 2011
NISTIR 7693	Specification for Asset Identification 1.1	May 2011
NISTIR 7692	Specification for the Open Checklist Interactive Language (OCIL) Version 2.0	April 2011
NISTIR 7682	Information System Security Best Practices for UOCAVA-Supporting Systems	August 2011
NISTIR 7298 Revision 1	Glossary of Key Information Security Terms	February 2011
NISTIR 7275 Revision 4	Specification for the Extensible Configuration Checklist Description Format (XCCDF) Version 1.2	September 2011

ITL SECURITY BULLETINS

Release Date	Title
September 2011	Managing the Configuration of Information Systems with a Focus on Security
August 2011	Protecting Industrial Control Systems - Key Components of our Nation's Critical Infrastructures
June 2011	Guidelines for Protecting Basic Input/Output System (Bios) Firmware
May 2011	Using Security Configuration Checklists and the National Checklist Program
April 2011	Full Virtualization Technologies: Guidelines for Secure Implementation and Management
March 2011	Managing Information Security Risk: Organization, Mission and Information System View
January 2011	Internet Protocol Version 6 (Ipv6): NIST Guidelines Help Organizations Manage the Secure Deployment of the New Network Protocol
December 2010	Securing WiMAX Wireless Communications
November 2010	The Exchange of Health Information: Designing a Security Architecture to Provide Information Security and Privacy
October 2010	Cyber Security Strategies for the Smart Grid: Protecting the Advanced Digital Infrastructure for Electric Power

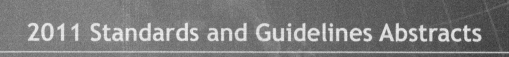

2011 Standards and Guidelines Abstracts

Federal Information Processing Standards (FIPS)

FIPS 201-2 (DRAFT): *Personal Identity Verification of Federal Employees and Contractors*
Group: Systems and Emerging Technologies Security Research

This standard specifies the architecture and technical requirements for a common identification standard for federal employees and contractors. The overall goal is to achieve appropriate security assurance for multiple applications by efficiently verifying the claimed identity of individuals seeking physical access to federally controlled government facilities and electronic access to government information systems.

The standard contains the minimum requirements for a federal personal identity verification system that meets the control and security objectives of Homeland Security Presidential Directive 12, including identity proofing, registration, and issuance. The standard also provides detailed specifications that will support technical interoperability among PIV systems of federal departments and agencies. It describes the card elements, system interfaces, and security controls required to securely store, process, and retrieve identity credentials from the card.

Contacts:
Ms. Hildegard Ferraiolo   Mr. William MacGregor
hildegard.ferraiolo@nist.gov

FIPS 180-4 (DRAFT): *Secure Hash Standard (SHS)*
Group: Cryptographic Technology

This standard specifies hash algorithms that can be used to generate digests of messages. The digests are used to detect whether messages have been changed since the digests were generated.

Contact:
Ms. Shu-jen Chang
shu-jen.chang@nist.gov

Special Publications (SP)

SP 800-153 (DRAFT): *Guidelines for Securing Wireless Local Area Networks (WLANs)*
Group: Systems and Emerging Technologies Security Research

The purpose of this publication is to provide organizations with recommendations for improving the security configuration and monitoring of their IEEE 802.11 wireless local area networks (WLANs) and their devices connecting to those networks.

This publication supplements other NIST publications by consolidating and strengthening their key recommendations, and it points readers to the appropriate NIST publications for additional information (see Appendix C for the full list of references and Appendix A for a list of major security controls relevant for WLAN security). The publication does not eliminate the need to follow recommendations in other NIST publications, such as [SP800-48] and [SP800-97]. If there is a conflict between recommendations in this publication and another NIST wireless publication, the recommendation in this publication takes precedence.

Contact:
Mr. Murugiah Souppaya
murugiah.souppaya@nist.gov

SP 800-147: *Basic Input/Output System (BIOS) Protection Guidelines*
Group: Cryptographic Technology

This document provides guidelines for preventing the unauthorized modification of BIOS firmware on PC client systems. Unauthorized modification of BIOS firmware by malicious software constitutes a significant threat because of the BIOS's unique and privileged position within the PC architecture. A malicious BIOS modification can result in installation of an advanced persistent threat (APT)—either a permanent denial of service (if the BIOS is corrupted) or a persistent malware presence (if the BIOS is implanted with malware).

Contacts:
Mr. David Cooper   Mr. William (Tim) Polk
david.cooper@nist.gov   william.polk@nist.gov

Mr. Andrew Regenscheid   Mr. Murugiah Souppaya
andrew.regenscheid@nist.gov   murugiah.souppaya@nist.gov

SP 800-146 (DRAFT): *Cloud Computing Synopsis and Recommendations*
Group: *Systems and Emerging Technologies*
Security Research

The purpose of this document is to provide recommendations for information technology decision makers, and to explain the cloud computing technology area in plain terms.

Cloud computing is a developing area, and its ultimate strengths and weaknesses are not yet fully researched, documented, and tested. This document presents what is known, gives recommendations on how and when cloud computing is an appropriate tool, and indicates the limits of current knowledge and areas for future analysis.

Contacts:
Mr. Lee Badger   Mr. Tim Grance
mark.badger@nist.gov   grance@nist.gov

Mr. Jeff Voas
jeff.voas@nist.gov

SP 800-145: *The NIST Definition of Cloud Computing*
Group: *Systems and Emerging Technologies*
Security Research

Cloud computing is an evolving paradigm. The NIST definition characterizes important aspects of cloud computing and is intended to serve as a means for broad comparisons of cloud services and deployment strategies, and to provide a baseline for discussion from what is cloud computing to how to best use cloud computing. The service and deployment models defined form a simple taxonomy that is not intended to prescribe or constrain any particular method of deployment, service delivery, or business operation.

Contacts:
Mr. Peter Mell   Mr. Tim Grance
peter.mell@nist.gov   grance@nist.gov

SP 800-144 (DRAFT): *Guidelines on Security and Privacy in Public Cloud Computing*
Group: *Systems and Emerging Technologies*
Security Research

The purpose of this document is to provide an overview of public cloud computing and the security and privacy challenges involved. The document discusses the threats, technology risks, and safeguards for public cloud environments, and provides the insight needed to make informed information technology decisions on their treatment.

Contact:
Mr. Tim Grance
grance@nist.gov

SP 800-142: *Practical Combinatorial Testing*
Group: *Systems and Emerging Technologies*
Security Research

This publication introduces combinatorial testing and explains how to use it effectively for system and software assurance.

Contact:
Mr. Richard Kuhn
rkuhn@nist.gov

SP 800-137: *Information Security Continuous Monitoring (ISCM) for Federal Information Systems and Organizations*
Group: *Security Management and Assurance*

The purpose of this guideline is to assist organizations in the development of a continuous monitoring strategy and the implementation of a continuous monitoring program providing visibility into organizational assets, awareness of threats and vulnerabilities, and visibility into the effectiveness of deployed security controls. It provides ongoing assurance that planned and implemented security controls are aligned with organizational risk tolerance as well as the information needed to respond to risk in a timely manner should observations indicate that the security controls are inadequate.

Contacts:
Ms. Kelley Dempsey   Mr. Arnold Johnson
kelley.dempsey@nist.gov   arnold.johnson@nist.gov

Mr. Kevin Stine   Mr. Matthew Scholl
kevin.stine@nist.gov   matthew.scholl@nist.gov

SP 800-135: *Recommendation for Existing Application-Specific Key Derivation Functions*
Group: Cryptographic Technology

Cryptographic keys are vital to the security of Internet security applications and protocols. Many widely used Internet security protocols have their own application-specific Key Derivation Functions (KDFs) that are used to generate the cryptographic keys required for their cryptographic functions. This recommendation provides security requirements for those KDFs.

Contact:
Mr. Quynh Dang
quynh.dang@nist.gov

SP 800-133 (DRAFT): *Recommendations for Cryptographic Key Generation*
Group: Cryptographic Technology

Cryptography is often used in an information technology security environment to protect data that is sensitive, has a high value, or is vulnerable to unauthorized disclosure or undetected modification during transmission or while in storage. Cryptography relies upon two basic components: an algorithm (or cryptographic methodology) and a cryptographic key. This recommendation discusses the generation of the keys to be managed and used by the approved cryptographic algorithms.

Contacts:
Ms. Elaine Barker
elaine.barker@nist.gov

Mr. Allen Roginsky
allen.roginsky@nist.gov

SP 800-132: *Recommendation for Password-Based Key Derivation Part 1: Storage Applications*
Group: Cryptographic Technology

This recommendation specifies techniques for the derivation of master keys from passwords or passphrases to protect stored electronic data or data protection keys.

Contacts:
Ms. Elaine Barker
elaine.barker@nist.gov

Ms. Lily Chen
lily.chen@nist.gov

SP 800-131A: *Transitions: Recommendation for Transitioning the Use of Cryptographic Algorithms and Key Lengths*
Group: Cryptographic Technology

At the start of the 21st century, the National Institute of Standards and Technology (NIST) began the task of providing cryptographic key management guidance, which includes defining and implementing appropriate key management procedures, using algorithms that adequately protect sensitive information, and planning ahead for possible changes in the use of cryptography because of algorithm breaks or the availability of more powerful computing techniques. NIST Special Publication (SP) 800-57, Part 1 was the first document produced in this effort, and includes a general approach for transitioning from one algorithm or key length to another. SP 800-131A provides more specific guidance for transitions to the use of stronger cryptographic keys and more robust algorithms.

Contacts:
Ms. Elaine Barker
elaine.barker@nist.gov

Mr. Allen Roginsky
allen.roginsky@nist.gov

SP 800-131B (DRAFT): *Transitions: Validation of Transitioning Cryptographic Algorithm and Key Lengths*
Group: Cryptographic Technology

At the start of the 21st century, NIST began the task of providing cryptographic key management guidance, which includes defining and implementing appropriate key management procedures, using algorithms that adequately protect sensitive information, and planning ahead for possible changes in the use of cryptography because of algorithm breaks or the availability of more powerful computing techniques. SP 800-57, Part 1, was the first document produced in this effort and includes a general approach for transitioning from one algorithm or key length to another. SP 800-131A provided more specific guidance for transitions to the use of stronger cryptographic keys and more robust algorithms. This document (SP 800-131B) is intended to provide more detail about the validation of the cryptographic algorithms and cryptographic modules in transition, as specified in SP 800-131A.

Contacts:
Ms. Elaine Barker
elaine.barker@nist.gov

Mr. Allen Roginsky
allen.roginsky@nist.gov

Mr. Randy Easter
randall.easter@nist.gov

Ms. Sharon Keller
sharon.keller@nist.gov

SP 800-131C (DRAFT): *Transitions: Validating the Transition from FIPS 186-2 to FIPS 186-3*
Group: Cryptographic Technology

Federal Information Processing Standard (FIPS) 186-3, *Digital Signature Standard*, was approved in June 2009 to replace FIPS 186-2. This transition plan addresses both the cryptographic algorithm validations and the cryptographic module validations that are conducted by the Cryptographic Algorithm Validation Program (CAVP) and the Cryptographic Module Validation Program (CMVP), respectively.

Contacts:

Ms. Elaine Barker	Mr. Allen Roginsky
elaine.barker@nist.gov	allen.roginsky@nist.gov
Mr. Randy Easter	Ms. Sharon Keller
randall.easter@nist.gov	sharon.keller@nist.gov

SP 800-128: *Guide for Security-Focused Configuration Management of Information Systems*
Group: Security Management and Assurance

An information system is typically in a constant state of change in response to new or enhanced hardware and software capability, patches for correcting errors to existing components, new security threats, changing business functions, etc. Implementing information system changes almost always results in some adjustment to the system information security configuration baseline. To ensure that adjustments to the system configuration do not adversely affect the security of the information system, a well-defined security configuration management process is needed. This publication provides guidelines for organizations responsible for managing changes to security configurations of federal information system computing environments. This publication also provides supporting guidance for implementation of the Configuration Management (CM) family of security controls defined in SP 800-53, *Recommended Security Controls for Federal Information Systems and Organizations*.

Contacts:

Mr. Arnold Johnson	Ms. Kelley Dempsey
arnold.johnson@nist.gov	kelley.dempsey@nist.gov

SP 800-126 Revision 2: *The Technical Specification for the Security Content Automation Protocol (SCAP): SCAP Version 1.2*
Group: Systems and Emerging Technologies Security Research

This document provides the definitive technical specification for Version 1.1 of the Security Content Automation Protocol (SCAP). SCAP (pronounced ess-cap) consists of a suite of specifications for standardizing the format and nomenclature by which security software communicates information about software flaws and security configurations. The document defines requirements for creating and processing SCAP content. These requirements build on the requirements defined within the individual SCAP component specifications. Each new requirement pertains either to using multiple component specifications together or to further constraining one of the individual component specifications. The requirements within the individual component specifications are not repeated in this document; see those specifications to access their requirements.

Contact:

Mr. David Waltermire	Mr. Stephen Quinn
david.waltermire@nist.gov	stephen.quinn@nist.gov

SP 800-126 Revision 1: *The Technical Specification for the Security Content Automation Protocol (SCAP): SCAP Version 1.2*
Group: Systems and Emerging Technologies Security Research

Refer to abstract above (SP 800-126 Revision 2). Revision 1 was released in February 2011. There were some high-priority updates that needed to take place, hence leading to Revision 2, which was released in September 2011.

SP 800-125: *Guide to Security for Full Virtualization Technologies*
Group: Systems and Emerging Technologies Security Research

The purpose of SP 800-125 is to discuss the security concerns associated with full virtualization technologies for server and desktop virtualization, and to provide recommendations for addressing these concerns. Full virtualization technologies run one or more operating systems and their applications on top of virtual hardware. Full virtualization is used for operational efficiency, such as in cloud computing, and for allowing users to run applications for multiple operating systems on a single computer.

Contact:
Mr. Murugiah Souppaya
murugiah.souppaya@nist.gov

SP 800-121 Revision 1 (DRAFT): *Guide to Bluetooth Security*
Group: Systems and Emerging Technologies Security Research

The purpose of this document is to provide information to organizations on the security capabilities of Bluetooth and provide recommendations to organizations employing Bluetooth technologies on securing them effectively. The Bluetooth versions within the scope of this publication are versions 1.1, 1.2, 2.0 + Enhanced Data Rate (EDR), 2.1 + EDR, 3.0 + High Speed (HS), and 4.0 Low Energy (LE).

Contact:
Mr. David Ferraiolo
david.ferraiolo@nist.gov

SP 800-119: *Guidelines for the Secure Deployment of IPv6*
Group: Systems and Emerging Technologies Security Research

The purpose of *Guidelines for the Secure Deployment of IPv6* is to provide information security guidance to organizations that are planning to deploy IPv6 technologies or are simply seeking a better understanding of IPv6. The scope of this document encompasses the IPv6 protocol and related protocol specifications. IPv6-related security considerations are discussed with emphasis on deployment-related security concerns. The document also includes general guidance on secure IPv6 deployment and integration planning.

Contact:
Ms. Sheila Frankel
sheila.frankel@nist.gov

SP 800-107 Revision 1 (DRAFT): *Recommendation for Applications Using Approved Hash Algorithms*
Group: Cryptographic Technology

Cryptographic hash functions that compute a fixed-length message digest from arbitrary length messages are widely used for many purposes in information security.

This document provides security guidelines for achieving the required or desired security strengths when using cryptographic applications that employ the approved cryptographic hash functions specified in Federal Information Processing Standard (FIPS) 180-4. These include functions such as digital signature applications, Keyed-hash Message Authentication Codes (HMACs), and Hash-based Key Derivation Functions (Hash-based KDFs).

Contact:
Mr. Quynh Dang
quynh.dang@nist.gov

SP 800-90A (DRAFT): *Recommendation for Random Number Generation Using Deterministic Random Bit Generators*
Group: Cryptographic Technology

This recommendation specifies mechanisms for the generation of random bits using deterministic methods. The methods provided are based on hash functions, block cipher algorithms, or number theoretic problems.

Contacts:
Ms. Elaine Barker   Mr. John Kelsey
elaine.barker@nist.gov   john.kelsey@nist.gov

SP 800-82: *Guide to Industrial Control Systems (ICS) Security*
Group: Security Management and Assurance

SP 800-82, *Guide to Industrial Control Systems (ICS) Security*, provides guidance on how to secure Industrial Control Systems (ICS), including Supervisory Control and Data Acquisition (SCADA) systems, Distributed Control Systems (DCS), and other control system configurations such as Programmable Logic Controllers (PLC), while addressing their unique performance, reliability, and safety requirements. SP 800-82 provides an overview of ICS and typical system topologies, identifies typical threats and vulnerabilities to these systems, and provides recommended security countermeasures to mitigate the associated risks.

Contacts:
Mr. Keith Stouffer   Dr. Ron Ross
keith.stouffer@nist.gov   rross@nist.gov

SP 800-78-3: *Cryptographic Algorithms and Key Sizes for Personal Identity Verification*
Group: Cryptographic Technology

The scope of this recommendation encompasses the PIV Card, infrastructure components that support issuance and management of the PIV Card, and applications that rely on the credentials supported by the PIV Card to provide security services. The recommendation identifies acceptable symmetric and asymmetric encryption algorithms, digital signature algorithms, key establishment schemes, and message digest algorithms, and specifies mechanisms to identify the algorithms associated with PIV keys or digital signatures.

Algorithms and key sizes have been selected for consistency with applicable federal standards and to ensure adequate cryptographic strength for PIV applications. All cryptographic algorithms employed in this specification provide at least 80 bits of security strength. For detailed guidance on the strength of cryptographic algorithms, see [SP800-57(1)], *Recommendation on Key Management – Part 1: General.*

Contacts:

Mr. William Polk
william.polk@nist.gov

Mr. David Cooper
david.cooper@nist.gov

Ms. Hildegard Ferraiolo
hferraiolo@nist.gov

SP 800-76-2 (DRAFT): *Biometric Data Specification for Personal Identity Verification*
Group: Systems and Emerging Technologies
Security Research

FIPS 201, *Personal Identity Verification (PIV) for Federal Employees and Contractors*, defines procedures for the PIV life-cycle activities including identity proofing, registration, PIV Card issuance and re-issuance, chain-of-trust operations, and PIV Card usage. FIPS 201 also defines the structure of an identity credential which includes biometric data. Requirements on interfaces are described in SP 800-73. Those on cryptographic protection of the biometric data are described in FIPS 201 and in SP 800-78.

This document contains technical specifications for biometric data mandated or allowed in FIPS 201. These specifications reflect the design goals of interoperability, performance, and security of the PIV Card and PIV processes. This specification addresses image acquisition to support the background check, fingerprint template creation, retention, and authentication. The goals are addressed by normatively citing biometric standards and by enumerating requirements where the standards include

options and branches. In such cases, a biometric profile can be used to declare what content is required and what is optional. This document goes further by constraining implementers' interpretation of the standards. Such restrictions are designed to ease implementation, assure conformity, facilitate interoperability, and ensure performance, in a manner tailored for PIV applications.

Contacts:

Mr. Patrick Grother
patrick.grother@nist.gov

Ms. Hildegard Ferraiolo
hildegard.ferraiolo@nist.gov

SP 800-70 Revision 2: *National Checklist Program for IT Products Guidelines for Checklist Users and Developers*
Group: Systems and Emerging Technologies
Security Research

This document describes security configuration checklists and their benefits, and explains how to use the NIST National Checklist Program (NCP) to find and retrieve checklists. The document also describes the policies, procedures, and general requirements for participation in the NCP.

Contacts:

Mr. Stephen Quinn
stephen.quinn@nist.gov

Mr. Murugiah Souppaya
murugiah.souppaya@nist.gov

SP 800-67 Revision 1 (DRAFT): *Recommendation for the Triple Data Encryption Algorithm (TDEA) Block Cipher*
Group: Cryptographic Technology

This publication specifies the Triple Data Encryption Algorithm (TDEA), including its primary component cryptographic engine, the Data Encryption Algorithm (DEA). When implemented in an SP 800-38 series-compliant mode of operation and in a FIPS 140-2-compliant cryptographic module, TDEA may be used by federal organizations to protect sensitive unclassified data. Protection of data during transmission or while in storage may be necessary to maintain the confidentiality and integrity of the information represented by the data. This recommendation defines the mathematical steps required to cryptographically protect data using TDEA and to subsequently process such protected data. The TDEA is made available for use by federal agencies within the context of a total security program consisting of physical security procedures, good information management practices, and computer system/network access controls.

Contact:
    Ms. Elaine Barker
    elaine.barker@nist.gov

SP 800-63, Revision 1 (Third DRAFT): *Electronic Authentication Guideline*
Group: Cryptographic Technology

This recommendation provides technical guidelines for federal agencies implementing electronic authentication, and it is not intended to constrict the development or use of standards outside of this purpose. The recommendation covers remote authentication of users over open networks. It defines technical requirements for each of four levels of assurance in the areas of identity proofing, registration, tokens, management processes, authentication protocols, and related assertions.

Contacts:
    Ms. Elaine Newton   Mr. Ray Perlner
    elaine.newton@nist.gov   ray.perlner@nist.gov

    Mr. Tim Polk
    william.polk@nist.gov

SP 800-57, Part 1 (DRAFT): *Recommendation for Key Management: Part 1: General*
Group: Cryptographic Technology

This recommendation provides cryptographic key management guidance. It consists of three parts. Part 1 provides general guidance and best practices for the management of cryptographic keying material. Part 2 provides guidance on policy and security planning requirements for U.S. government agencies. Finally, Part 3 provides guidance when using the cryptographic features of current systems.

Contacts:
    Ms. Elaine Barker   Mr. William Polk
    elaine.barker@nist.gov   william.polk@nist.gov

SP 800-56C (Second DRAFT): *Recommendation for Key Derivation through Extraction-then-Expansion*
Group: Cryptographic Technology

This recommendation specifies techniques for the derivation of keying material from a shared secret established during a key establishment scheme defined in SPs 800-56A or 800-56B through an extraction-then-expansion procedure.

Contact:
    Ms. Lily Chen
    lily.chen@nist.gov

SP 800-53 Appendix J (DRAFT): *Privacy Control Catalog*
Group: Security Management and Assurance

Appendix J, *Privacy Control Catalog*, is a new addition to NIST's family of standards and guidelines that will be incorporated into the 2011 update to Special Publication 800-53, Revision 4, projected for release in December 2011. Due to the importance and special nature of the material in this Appendix, it is being publicly vetted separately from the other changes to the publication which will be released later this year. The objectives of the Privacy Appendix are fourfold:

- Provide a structured set of privacy controls, based on international standards and best practices, that help organizations enforce requirements deriving from federal privacy legislation, policies, regulations, directives, standards, and guidance;

- Establish a linkage and relationship between privacy and security controls for purposes of enforcing respective privacy and security requirements which may overlap in concept and in implementation within federal information systems, programs, and organizations;

- Demonstrate the applicability of the NIST Risk Management Framework in the selection, implementation, assessment, and monitoring of privacy controls deployed in federal information systems, programs, and organizations; and

- Promote closer cooperation between privacy and security officials within the federal government to help achieve the objectives of senior leaders/ executives in enforcing the requirements in federal privacy legislation, policies, regulations, directives, standards, and guidance.

Contact:
    Dr. Ron Ross
    rross@nist.gov

SP 800-51 Revision 1: *Guide to Using Vulnerability Naming Schemes*
Group: Systems and Emerging Technologies Security Research

This publication provides recommendations for using two vulnerability naming schemes: Common Vulnerabilities and Exposures (CVE) and Common Configuration Enumeration (CCE). Draft SP 800-51 Revision 1 gives an introduction to both naming schemes and makes recommendations for end-user organizations on using their names. The publication also presents recommendations for software and service vendors on how they should use vulnerability names and naming schemes in their product and service offerings.

Contact:
Mr. David Waltermire
david.waltermire@nist.gov

SP 800-39: *Managing Information Security Risk: Organization, Mission, and Information System View*
Group: Security Management and Assurance

SP 800-39 is the flagship document in the series of information security standards and guidelines developed by NIST in response to FISMA. The purpose of Special Publication 800-39 is to provide guidance for an integrated, organization-wide program for managing information security risk to organizational operations (i.e., mission, functions, image, and reputation), organizational assets, individuals, other organizations, and the Nation resulting from the operation and use of federal information systems. Special Publication 800-39 provides a structured, yet flexible approach for managing risk that is intentionally broad-based, with the specific details of assessing, responding to, and monitoring risk on an ongoing basis provided by other supporting NIST security standards and guidelines. The guidance provided in this publication is not intended to replace or subsume other risk-related activities, programs, processes, or approaches that organizations have implemented or intend to implement addressing areas of risk management covered by other legislation, directives, policies, programmatic initiatives, or mission/business requirements. Rather, the risk management guidance described herein is complementary to and should be used as part of a more comprehensive Enterprise Risk Management (ERM) program.

Contacts:
Dr. Ron Ross
rross@nist.gov

Mr. Arnold Johnson
arnold.johnson@nist.gov

Ms. Marianne Swanson
marianne.swanson@nist.gov

SP 800-38 A – Addendum: *Recommendation for Block Cipher Modes of Operation: Three Variants of Ciphertext Stealing for CBC Mode*
Group: Cryptographic Technology

A limitation to Cipher Block Chaining (CBC) mode, as specified in SP 800-38A, Ref. [1], is that the plaintext input must consist of a sequence of blocks. (In the rest of this publication, a block is called a "complete block" to emphasize the contrast with a "partial block" whose bit length is smaller than the block size.) Although Appendix A of Ref. [1] describes how padding methods can be used to meet this requirement, in such cases, the length of the resulting ciphertext expands over the length of the unpadded plaintext by the number of padding bits.

This addendum to Ref. [1] specifies three variants of CBC mode that accept any plaintext input whose bit length is greater than or equal to the block size, whether or not the length is a multiple of the block size. Unlike the padding methods discussed in Ref. [1], these variants avoid ciphertext expansion.

Contact:
Mr. Morris Dworkin
morris.dworkin@nist.gov

SP 800-38F (DRAFT): *Recommendation for Block Cipher Modes of Operation: Methods for Key Wrapping*
Group: Cryptographic Technology

This publication is the sixth part in a series of recommendations regarding the modes of operation of block cipher algorithms. The purpose of this part is to provide approved methods for key wrapping, i.e., the protection of cryptographic keys.

This publication describes cryptographic methods that are approved for "key wrapping," i.e., the protection of the confidentiality and integrity of cryptographic keys. In addition to describing existing methods, this publication specifies two new deterministic authenticated encryption modes of operation of the Advanced Encryption Standard (AES) algorithm: the AES Key Wrap (KW) mode and the AES Key Wrap With Padding (KWP) mode. The analogous mode with the Triple Data Encryption Algorithm (TDEA) as the underlying block cipher, called TKW, is also specified, to support legacy applications.

Contact:
Mr. Morris Dworkin
morris.dworkin@nist.gov

SP 800-30 Revision 1 (DRAFT): *Guide for Conducting Risk Assessments*
Group: Security Management and Assurance

The purpose of Special Publication 800-30 is to provide guidance for conducting risk assessments of federal information systems and organizations. Risk assessments, carried out at all three tiers in the risk management hierarchy, are part of an overall risk management process—providing senior leaders/executives with the information needed to determine appropriate courses of action to take in response to identified risks. In particular, this document provides practitioners with practical guidance for carrying out each of the three steps in the risk assessment process (i.e., prepare for the assessment, conduct the assessment, and maintain the assessment) and how risk assessments and other organizational risk management processes complement and inform each other. Special Publication 800-30 also provides guidance on identifying risk factors to monitor on an ongoing basis, so that organizations can determine whether levels of risk have increased to unacceptable levels (i.e., exceeding organizational risk tolerance) and different courses of action should be taken.

Contacts:

Dr. Ron Ross
rross@nist.gov

Mr. Arnold Johnson
arnold.johnson@nist.gov

Ms. Kelley Dempsey
kelley.dempsey@nist.gov

NIST Interagency Reports (NIST IRs)

NISTIR 7806: *ANSI/NIST-ITL 1-2011 Requirements and Conformance Test Assertions*
Group: Systems and Emerging Technologies Security Research

The current version of the ANSI/NIST-ITL standard "Data Format for the Interchange of Fingerprint, Facial & Other Biometric Information" is specified in two parts. Part 1, ANSI/NIST-ITL 1-2007, specifies the traditional format, and Part 2, ANSI/NIST-ITL 2-2008, specifies a NIEM-conformant XML format. Both parts have been combined into one document, which is being revised and augmented. The Computer Security Division (CSD) of NIST/ITL has developed a set of test assertions based on the requirements specified in the 4th draft of the new ANSI/NIST-ITL standard. Over 1,200 test assertions have been identified and organized into a set of tables to assist in the development of a conformance test tool designed to test implementations of the new version of the ANSI/NIST-ITL standard for selected record types. These tables were contributed to the Conformance Testing Methodology (CTM) Working Group which was recently established by NIST/ITL to develop a CTM for the new version of the ANSI/NIST-ITL (AN-2011) standard. A ballot was conducted on a revised draft (5th draft) of the AN-2011 standard. A new draft will be developed based on the comments received as a result of this ballot. As the technical content of the AN-2011 draft standard evolves towards approval and publication, and comments on the assertion tables in this document are received, revised versions of these tables will be developed until they fully address the requirements of the approved AN-2011 standard. This publication documents the assertions developed and the terms, operands, and operators used in defining these assertions. Brief information on previous and ongoing conformance test tools development within NIST/ITL CSD is included.

Contacts:

Mr. Fernando Podio
fernando.podio@nist.gov

Mr. Dylan Yaga
dylan.yaga@nist.gov

NISTIR 7802: *Trust Model for Security Automation Data 1.0 (TMSAD)*
Group: Systems and Emerging Technologies Security Research

This report defines the Trust Model for Security Automation Data 1.0 (TMSAD), which permits users to establish integrity, authentication, and traceability for security automation data. Since security automation data is primarily stored and exchanged using Extensible Markup Language (XML) documents, the focus of the trust model is on the processing of XML documents. The trust model is composed of recommendations on how to use existing specifications to represent signatures, hashes, key information, and identity information in the context of an XML document within the security automation domain.

Contact

Mr. Harold Booth
harold.booth@nist.gov

NISTIR 7791: *Conformance Test Architecture and Test Suite for ANSI/NIST-ITL 1-2007*
Group: Systems and Emerging Technologies
Security Research

The Computer Security Division of NIST/ITL supports the development of biometric conformance testing methodology standards and other conformity assessment efforts through active technical participation in the development of these standards and the associated conformance test architectures and test suites. The ANSI/NIST-ITL standard "Data Format for the Interchange of Fingerprint, Facial & Other Biometric Information" is used by law enforcement, intelligence, military, and homeland security organizations throughout the world. The current version specified in its Traditional Format, is Part 1: ANSI/NIST-ITL 1-2007. Although a revised and augmented version of the standard is under development, the 2007 version is still widely used. The Conformance Test Architecture and Test Suite described in this publication are designed to test implementations of ANSI/NIST ITL 1-2007. The code (Beta 0.4) is currently designed to support testing of selected record types of the standard but can be extended to support other record types as required. A high-level overview of the architecture and test suite as well as software details and the code structure are provided. A quick-start user guide and a comprehensive table of the standard's requirements and the associated implemented conformance test assertions (over 530) are included.

Contacts:

Mr. Fernando Podio
fernando.podio@nist.gov

Mr. Dylan Yaga
dylan.yaga@nist.gov

NISTIR 7788: *Security Risk Analysis of Enterprise Networks Using Probabilistic Attack Graphs*
Group: Systems and Emerging Technologies
Security Research

Today's information systems face sophisticated attackers who combine multiple vulnerabilities to penetrate networks with devastating impact. The overall security of an enterprise network cannot be determined by simply counting the number of vulnerabilities. To accurately assess the security of enterprise systems, one must understand how vulnerabilities can be combined to stage an attack. We model such composition of vulnerabilities through probabilistic attack graphs, which show all paths of attacks that allow incremental network penetration.

We propagate attack likelihoods through the attack graph, yielding a novel way to measure the security risk of enterprise systems. We use this metric for risk mitigation analysis to maximize the security of enterprise systems. We believe that our methodology based on probabilistic attack graphs can be used to evaluate and strengthen the overall security of enterprise networks.

Contact:

Dr. Anoop Singhal
anoop.singhal@nist.gov

NISTIR 7773: *An Application of Combinatorial Methods to Conformance Testing for Document Object Model Events*
Group: Systems and Emerging Technologies
Security Research

This report describes the use of combinatorial test methods to reduce the cost of testing for the Document Object Model Events standard while maintaining an equivalent level of assurance. More than 36,000 tests – all possible combinations of equivalence class values –were reduced by approximately a factor of 20 with no reduction in error detection effectiveness.

Contact:

Mr. Richard Kuhn
rkuhn@nist.gov

NISTIR 7771: *Conformance Test Architecture for Biometric Data Interchange Formats - Version Beta 2.0*
Group: Systems and Emerging Technologies
Security Research

The success of biometric applications is particularly dependent on the interoperability of biometric systems. Deploying these systems requires a comprehensive portfolio of biometric standards developed in support of interoperability and data interchange. A number of these domestic and international standards have been published and others are under development. The existence of these standards alone is not enough to demonstrate that products meet the technical requirements specified in the standards. Conformance testing captures the technical description of a specification and measures whether an implementation faithfully implements the specification. The Computer Security Division of NIST/ITL supports conformity assessment efforts through active technical participation in the development of conformance testing methodology standards and the development of associated conformance test architectures (CTAs) and test suites (CTSs). This NISTIR discusses the technological characteristics of the recently released CTA Beta 2.0. This architecture supports CTSs such as those designed to test implementations of biometric data interchange data formats. The information provided includes CTA module communication methods, key CTA features and high-level sequence diagrams such as testing and decoding operations. It also addresses an introduction to testing binary data, structure testing by groups of fields, and a discussion on test cases. Ongoing work on related tools development is also presented.

Contacts:

Mr. Fernando Podio
fernando.podio@nist.gov

Mr. Dylan Yaga
dylan.yaga@nist.gov

NISTIR 7770: *Security Considerations for Remote Electronic UOCAVA Voting*
Group: *Cryptographic Technology*

This document outlines the basic process for the distribution of election material including registration material and blank ballots to the Uniformed and Oversea Citizens Absentee Voting Act (UOCAVA) voters. It describes the technologies that can be used to support the electronic dissemination of election material along with security techniques – both technical and procedural – that can protect this transfer. The purpose of the document is to inform Election Officials about the current technologies and techniques that can be used to improve the delivery of election material for UOCAVA voters. This document is part of a series of documents that address the UOCAVA voting. The first NIST publication on UOCAVA voting, NISTIR 7551, *A Threat Analysis on UOCAVA Voting Systems*, was released in December 2008. In addition to NISTIR 7551, NIST has released NISTIR 7770, *Security Considerations for Remote Electronic UOCAVA Voting, Accessibility and Usability Considerations for Remote Electronic UOCAVA Voting*, and NISTIR 7682, *Information Systems Security Best Practices for UOCAVA-Supporting Systems*.

Contact:

Mr. Andrew Regenscheid
andrew.regenscheid@nist.gov

NISTIR 7764: *Status Report on the Second Round of the SHA-3 Cryptographic Hash Algorithm Competition*
Group: *Cryptographic Technology*

NIST opened a public competition on November 2, 2007, to develop a new cryptographic hash algorithm - SHA-3, which will augment the hash algorithms currently specified in Federal Information Processing Standard (FIPS) 180-3, *Secure Hash Standard*. The competition was NIST's response to advances in the cryptanalysis of hash algorithms. NIST received 64 submissions in October 2008, and selected 51 candidate algorithms as the first-round candidates on December 10, 2008, and 14 as the second-round candidates on July 24, 2009. One year was allocated for the public review of the second-round candidates. On December 9, 2010, NIST announced five SHA-3 finalists to advance to the third (and final) round of the competition. This report summarized the evaluation and selection of the five finalists - BLAKE, Grøstl, JH, Keccak, and Skein.

Contacts:

Ms. Shu-jen Chang
shu-jen.chang@nist.gov

Mr. Ray Perlner
ray.perlner@nist.gov

Mr. Larry Bassham
lawrence.bassham@nist.gov

Mr. Morris Dworkin
morris.dworkin@nist.gov

Mr. John Kelsey
john.kelsey@nist.gov

Mr. Rene Peralta
rene.peralta@nist.gov

NISTIR 7756 (DRAFT): *CAESARS Framework Extension: An Enterprise Continuous Monitoring Technical Reference Architecture*
Group: *Systems and Emerging Technologies Security Research*

This publication and its supporting documents present an enterprise continuous monitoring technical reference model that extends the framework provided by the DHS Federal Network Security CAESARS architecture. This extension enables added functionality, defines each subsystem in more detail, and further leverages security automation standards. It also extends CAESARS to allow for large implementations that need a multi-tier architecture and focuses on the necessary inter-tier communications. The goal of this document is to facilitate enterprise continuous monitoring by presenting a reference model that enables organizations to aggregate collected data from across a diverse set of security tools, analyze that data, perform scoring, enable user queries, and provide overall situational awareness. The model design is focused on enabling organizations to realize this capability by leveraging their existing security tools and thus avoiding complicated and resource-intensive custom tool integration efforts.

Contacts:

Mr. David Waltermire
david.waltermire@nist.gov

Mr. Peter Mell
peter.mell@nist.gov

Mr. Harold Booth
harold.booth@nist.gov

NISTIR 7751: *2010 Annual Report, Computer Security Division*
Group: Security Management and Assurance

This annual report covers the work conducted within the National Institute of Standards and Technology's Computer Security Division during Fiscal Year 2010 (October 1, 2009 to September 30, 2010). It discusses all projects and programs within the division, staff highlights, and publications.

Contacts:

Mr. Patrick O'Reilly
patrick.oreilly@nist.gov

Mr. Kevin Stine
kevin.stine@nist.gov

NISTIR 7711: *Security Best Practices for the Electronic Transmission of Election Materials for UOCAVA Voters*
Group: Cryptographic Technology

This document outlines the basic process for the distribution of election material including registration material and blank ballots to UOCAVA voters. It describes the technologies that can be used to support the electronic dissemination of election material along with security techniques – both technical and procedural – that can protect this transfer. The purpose of the document is to inform Election Officials about the current technologies and techniques that can be used to improve the delivery of election material for UOCAVA voters. This document is part of a series of documents that address the UOCAVA voting. The first NIST publication on UOCAVA voting, entitled NISTIR 7551, *A Threat Analysis on UOCAVA Voting Systems*, was released in December 2008. In addition to NISTIR 7551, NIST has released NISTIR 7770, *Security Considerations for Remote Electronic UOCAVA Voting, Accessibility and Usability Considerations for Remote Electronic UOCAVA Voting*, and NISTIR 7682, *Information Systems Security Best Practices for UOCAVA-Supporting Systems*.

Contact:

Mr. Andrew Regenscheid
andrew.regenscheid@nist.gov

NISTIR 7698: *Common Platform Enumeration: Applicability Language Specification Version 2.3*
Group: Systems and Emerging Technologies Security Research

This report defines the Common Platform Enumeration (CPE) Applicability Language version 2.3 specification. The CPE Applicability Language specification is part of a stack of CPE specifications that support a variety of use cases relating to IT product description and naming. The CPE Applicability Language data model builds on top of other CPE specifications to provide the functionality required to allow CPE users to construct complex groupings of CPE names to describe IT platforms. These groupings are referred to as applicability statements because they are used to designate which platforms particular guidance, policies, etc., apply to. This report defines the semantics of the CPE Applicability Language data model and the requirements that IT products and CPE Applicability Language documents must meet for conformance with the CPE Applicability Language version 2.3 specification.

Contacts:

Mr. David Waltermire
david.waltermire@nist.gov

Mr. Paul Cichonski
paul.cichonski@nist.gov

NISTIR 7697: *Common Platform Enumeration: Dictionary Specification Version 2.3*
Group: Systems and Emerging Technologies Security Research

This report defines the Common Platform Enumeration (CPE) Dictionary version 2.3 specification. The CPE Dictionary Specification is a part of a stack of CPE specifications that support a variety of use cases relating to IT product description and naming. An individual CPE dictionary is a repository of IT product names, with each name in the repository identifying a unique class of IT product in the world. This specification defines the semantics of the CPE Dictionary data model and the rules associated with CPE dictionary creation and management. The report also defines and explains the requirements that IT products and services, including CPE dictionaries, must meet for conformance with the CPE Dictionary version 2.3 specification.

Contacts:

Mr. David Waltermire
david.waltermire@nist.gov

Mr. Paul Cichonski
paul.cichonski@nist.gov

NISTIR 7696: *Common Platform Enumeration: Name Matching Specification Version 2.3*
Group: Systems and Emerging Technologies
Security Research

This report defines the Common Platform Enumeration (CPE) Name Matching version 2.3 specification. The CPE Name Matching specification is part of a stack of CPE specifications that support a variety of use cases relating to IT product description and naming. The CPE Name Matching specification provides a method for conducting a one-to-one comparison of a source CPE name to a target CPE name. In addition to defining the specification, the report also defines and explains the requirements that IT products must meet for conformance with the CPE Name Matching version 2.3 specification.

Contacts:
Mr. David Waltermire   Mr. Harold Booth
david.waltermire@nist.gov   harold.booth@nist.gov

NISTIR 7695: *Common Platform Enumeration: Naming Specification Version 2.3*
Group: Systems and Emerging Technologies
Security Research

This report defines the Common Platform Enumeration (CPE) Naming version 2.3 specification. The CPE Naming specification is a part of a stack of CPE specifications that support a variety of use cases relating to IT product description and naming. The CPE Naming specification defines the logical structure of names for IT product classes and the procedures for binding and unbinding these names to and from machine-readable encodings. The report also defines and explains the requirements that IT products must meet for conformance with the CPE Naming version 2.3 specification.

Contact:
Mr. David Waltermire
david.waltermire@nist.gov

NISTIR 7694: *Specification for the Asset Reporting Format 1.1*
Group: Systems and Emerging Technologies
Security Research

This specification describes the Asset Reporting Format (ARF), a data model for expressing the transport format of information about assets and the relationships between assets and reports. The standardized data model facilitates the reporting, correlating, and fusing of asset information throughout and between organizations. ARF is vendor- and technology-neutral, flexible, and suited for a wide variety of reporting applications. The intent of ARF is to provide a uniform foundation for the expression of reporting results, fostering more widespread application of sound IT management practices. ARF can be used for any type of asset, not just IT assets.

Contact:
Mr. David Waltermire
david.waltermire@nist.gov

NISTIR 7693: *Specification for Asset Identification 1.1*
Group: Systems and Emerging Technologies
Security Research

Asset identification plays an important role in an organization's ability to quickly correlate different sets of information about assets. This specification provides the necessary constructs to uniquely identify assets based on known identifiers and/or known information about the assets. The specification describes the purpose of asset identification, a data model for identifying assets, methods for identifying assets, and guidance on how to use asset identification. It also identifies a number of known use cases for asset identification.

Contact:
Mr. David Waltermire
david.waltermire@nist.gov

NISTIR 7692: *Specification for the Open Checklist Interactive Language (OCIL) Version 2.0*
Group: Systems and Emerging Technologies Security Research

This report defines version 2.0 of the Open Checklist Interactive Language (OCIL). The intent of OCIL is to provide a standardized basis for expressing questionnaires and related information, such as answers to questions and final questionnaire results, so that the questionnaires can use a standardized, machine-readable approach to interacting with humans and using information stored during previous data collection efforts. OCIL documents are Extensible Markup Language (XML)-based. The report defines and explains the requirements that IT products and OCIL documents asserting conformance with the OCIL 2.0 specification must meet.

Contact:
  Mr. David Waltermire
  david.waltermire@nist.gov

NISTIR 7682: *Information System Security Best Practices for UOCAVA-Supporting Systems*
Group: Cryptographic Technology

IT systems used to support UOCAVA voting face a variety of threats. If IT systems are not selected, configured, and managed using security practices commensurate with the importance of the services they provide and the sensitivity of the data they handle, a security compromise could carry consequences for the integrity of the election and the confidentiality of sensitive voter information. Failure to adequately address threats to these systems could prevent voters from casting ballots, expose individuals to identity fraud, or even compromise the results of an election. This document offers procedural and technical guidance, along with references to additional resources, to assist jurisdictions with the secure deployment of these systems.

Contact:
  Mr. Andrew Regenscheid
  andrew.regenscheid@nist.gov

NISTIR 7670 (DRAFT): *Proposed Open Specifications for an Enterprise Remediation Automation Framework*
Group: Systems and Emerging Technologies Security Research

The success of SCAP in automated system assessment has fostered research related to the development of similar open specifications in support of enterprise remediation. Enterprise remediation is focused on delivering capabilities that allow organizations to identify, describe and implement desired system changes across the enterprise. Remediation actions can include changes to the configuration of an operating system or application, installation of a software patch, or the installation or removal of applications and libraries. This report examines technical use cases for enterprise remediation, identifies high-level requirements for these use cases, and proposes a set of emerging specifications that satisfy those requirements.

This report is a product of ongoing collaboration between the National Institute of Standards and Technology (NIST), the US Department of Defense, and the MITRE Corporation. Participation from a broader community of interested parties is actively sought to help define, refine and mature proposed remediation standards.

Contact:
  Mr. David Waltermire
  david.waltermire@nist.gov

NISTIR 7511 Revision 2: *Security Content Automation Protocol (SCAP) Version 1.0 Validation Program Test Requirements*
Group: Systems and Emerging Technologies Security Research

This report defines the requirements and associated test procedures necessary for products to achieve one or more Security Content Automation Protocol (SCAP) validations. Validation is awarded based on a defined set of SCAP capabilities by independent laboratories that have been accredited for SCAP testing by the NIST National Voluntary Laboratory Accreditation Program (NVLAP).

Contacts:
  Mr. David Waltermire   Mr. John Banghart
  david.waltermire@nist.gov   john.banghart@nist.gov

  Mr. Stephen Quinn
  stephen.quinn@nist.gov

NISTIR 7298 Revision 1: *Glossary of Key Information Security Terms*
Group: Security Management and Assurance

This glossary of key information security terms has been extracted from Federal Information Processing Standards (FIPS), Special Publication (SP) 800 series, NIST Interagency Report (NISTIR) series, and the Committee for National Security Systems Instruction (CNSSI) 4009 (Information Assurance Glossary). The terms included are not all-inclusive of terms found in these publications, but are a subset of those most frequently used. The purpose of this glossary is to provide a central resource of definitions most commonly used in NIST and CNSS publications. Each entry in the glossary points to one or more source NIST or CNSS publications, and in addition, other supplemental sources where appropriate. As we are continually refreshing out publication site, terms included in the glossary come from our more recent publications.

Contact:
Mr. Richard Kissel
richard.kissel@nist.gov

NISTIR 7275 Revision 4: *Specification for the Extensible Configuration Checklist Description Format (XCCDF) Version 1.2*
Group: Systems and Emerging Technologies Security Research

This report specifies the data model and Extensible Markup Language (XML) representation for the Extensible Configuration Checklist Description Format (XCCDF) Version 1.2. An XCCDF document is a structured collection of security configuration rules for some set of target systems. The XCCDF specification is designed to support information interchange, document generation, organizational and situational tailoring, automated compliance testing, and scoring. The specification also defines a data model and format for storing results of security guidance or checklist testing. The intent of XCCDF is to provide a uniform foundation for expression of security checklists and other configuration guidance, and thereby foster more widespread application of good security practices.

Contact:
Mr. Stephen Quinn
stephen.quinn@nist.gov

Ways to Engage Our Division and NIST

Guest Research Internships at NIST

Opportunities are available at NIST for 6- to 24-month internships within CSD. Qualified individuals should contact CSD, provide a statement of qualifications, and indicate the area of work that is of interest. Generally speaking, the salary costs are borne by the sponsoring institution; however, in some cases, these guest research internships carry a small monthly stipend paid by NIST. For further information, contact:

Ms. Donna Dodson, (301) 975-8443,
donna.dodson@nist.gov or
Mr. Matthew Scholl, (301) 975-2941,
matthew.scholl@nist.gov

Details at NIST for Government or Military Personnel

Opportunities are available at NIST for 6- to 24-month details at NIST in CSD. Qualified individuals should contact CSD, provide a statement of qualifications, and indicate the area of work that is of interest. Generally speaking, the salary costs are borne by the sponsoring agency; however, in some cases, agency salary costs may be reimbursed by NIST. For further information, contact:

Ms. Donna Dodson, (301) 975-8443,
donna.dodson@nist.gov or
Mr. Matthew Scholl, (301) 975-2941,
matthew.scholl@nist.gov

Federal Computer Security Program Managers' Forum (FCSPM)

The FCSPM Forum is covered in detail in the Outreach section of this report. Membership is free and open to federal employees. For further information, contact:

Mr. Kevin Stine, (301) 975-4483, kevin.stine@nist.gov
or visit the FCSPM Forum website at
http://csrc.nist.gov/groups/SMA/
forum/membership.html

Security Research

NIST occasionally undertakes security work, primarily in the area of research, funded by other agencies. Such sponsored work is accepted by NIST when it can cost-effectively further the goals of NIST and the sponsoring institution. For further information, contact:

Donna Dodson, Chief,
Computer Security Division, donna.dodson@nist.gov

Funding Opportunities at NIST

NIST funds industrial and academic research in a variety of ways. The Small Business Innovation Research Program funds R&D proposals from small businesses; see www.nist.gov/sbir. We also offer other grants to encourage work in specific fields: precision measurement, fire research, and materials science. Grants/awards supporting research at industry, academia, and other institutions are available on a competitive basis through several different Institute offices:

For general information on NIST grants programs, please contact:
Christopher Hunton at (301) 975-5718
or christopher.hunton@nist.gov.

Further details on funding opportunities may be found on http://www.nist.gov/director/ocfo/grants/grants.cfm

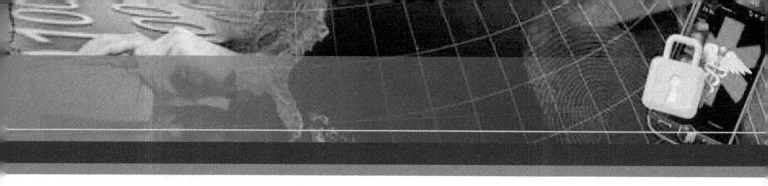

Summer Undergraduate Research Fellowship (SURF)

Curious about physics, electronics, manufacturing, chemistry, materials science, or structural engineering? Intrigued by nanotechnology, fire research, information technology, or robotics? Tickled by biotechnology or biometrics? Have an intellectual fancy for superconductors or perhaps semiconductors?

Here's your chance to satisfy that curiosity, by spending part of your summer working elbow-to-elbow with researchers at NIST, one of the world's leading research organizations and home to three Nobel Prize winners. Gain valuable hands-on experience, work with cutting-edge technology, and sample the Washington, D.C., area. And get paid while you're learning. Applications must be submitted by an academic institution (e.g., by the chair of an academic department or by appropriate administrative staff).

SURF is a partnership, supported by NIST, the National Science Foundation, and the participating colleges and universities. Additional information on student eligibility criteria, plan of operation, and contacts can be found through the website:

http://www.nist.gov/itl/itl-surf-program.cfm
or contact:
NIST SURF Program
100 Bureau Drive, Stop 8400
Gaithersburg, MD 20899-8499

Acknowledgements

Acknowledgements

The editor, Patrick O'Reilly of the Computer Security Division, wishes to thank his colleagues in the Computer Security Division, who provided write-ups on their 2011 project highlights and accomplishments for this annual report (their names are mentioned after each project write-up). The editor would also like to acknowledge Shirley Radack, Elizabeth Lennon, Lisa Carnahan, Kevin Stine, and Judy Barnard (all of NIST) for reviewing and providing feedback for this annual report.

Table of Contents

NIST
National Institute of
Standards and Technology
U.S. Department of Commerce

www.ingramcontent.com/pod-product-compliance
Lightning Source LLC
Chambersburg PA
CBHW080603060326
40689CB00021B/4915